For the
─────
LOVE *of* GOD

Handbook for the Spirit

For the

LOVE *of* GOD

Handbook for the Spirit

Edited by
BENJAMIN SHIELD, PH.D., AND
RICHARD CARLSON, PH.D.

NEW WORLD LIBRARY
NOVATO, CALIFORNIA

New World Library
14 Pamaron Way
Novato, California 94949

Revised Edition © 1997 Benjamin Shield, Ph.D.,
and Richard Carlson, Ph.D.
Original Edition © 1990 Benjamin Shield, Ph.D.,
and Richard Carlson, Ph.D.

Copyright notices for the writings by the contributors
are found at the back of this book.

Editorial: Jason Gardner and Carol LaRusso
Cover design: Nita Ybarra
Text design: Aaron Kenedi

Library of Congress Cataloging-in-Publication Data

For the love of God : handbook for the spirit /
edited by Benjamin Shield & Richard Carlson ;
foreword by Marianne Williamson. — Rev. ed.
p. cm.
ISBN 1-57731-061-6 (hardcover : alk. paper)
1. Spiritual biography. 2. Spiritual life. I. Shield, Benjamin, 1964– .
II. Carlson, Richard, 1961 May 16–
BL72.F57   1997
291.4—dc21   97-28695

CIP

First Printing, November 1997
Printed in the U.S.A. on acid-free paper
ISBN 1-57731-061-6
Distributed to the trade by Publishers Group West

10 9 8 7 6 5 4 3 2 1

To Our Parents

Contents

Acknowledgments

We would like to thank the participants of this anthology for the selfless gifts of their wisdom and time, and for demonstrating what presence and faith is all about. Special thanks to Don Carlson for his loving assistance, Tara Carson for her love, and to each other for proving that the best of friends can be the best of partners.

Preface

FOR THOSE ON A SPIRITUAL PATHWAY, editors Benjamin Shield and Richard Carlson have harnessed a magnificient variety of opinion by some of the world's best-known teachers. Although the authors come from a diversity of backgrounds, they had much in common when responding to questions about their relationships with God and with life.

For some people the word "God" is a limiting term, and for others it is a nonissue word. I was as moved by His Holiness the Dalai Lama's remarks, who did not use the word "God" in his writing, as I was by others who did write about God. The simplicity of His Holiness's remarks about the applications of kindness, compassion, and tolerance in our lives, the harmony between our hearts and our minds, and the importance of our spiritual sustenance are concepts that go directly to the core of our souls. What a wonderful blessing for the world that he was chosen to receive the Nobel Peace Prize for 1989.

I had the good fortune to spend time with His Holiness during the filming of a special television program on our project "Children as Teachers of Peace." Here was a human being who lived the principles he so eloquently taught. He demonstrated to everyone an experience of unconditional love, inner peace, joyfulness, kindness, compassion, tolerance, and the Oneness of the Universe.

We don't have to believe in God or use the word "God" to experience Oneness. The moment our ego and intellect come into play we attempt to categorize and put words around our concepts about God, a feeling of separation from one another often takes place. Yet, the beauty of this collection of spiritual wisdom by some of today's outstanding leaders shows how each, in an individual and heartfelt way, uses different words and different metaphors toward a common goal: to bring us together as a human family, celebrating our Oneness and not our separateness.

It is our thoughts, actions, and how we live and experience our lives that is important, not the words we use. When we believe that the essence of our being is love, that our true identity is a spiritual one, it becomes easier to understand that all our relationships offer us opportunities to experience that light of love in one another and to know that what we see is but a reflection of ourselves. Our experiences with that which Created us, which many people call "God," therefore becomes manifested by our relationships.

Although I am now comfortable using the word "God" with myself, I frankly am not totally at ease using it with others. People's perceptions of what that word means have differed so much, causing not only separation, but also many wars. When we give our total love to one another with no exceptions, however, we can then recognize that the purpose of all our relationships is to see the light of love in everyone we see. As you read this book, I hope you will find yourself rekindling the light that has always been in you.

Perhaps more joining and understanding will take place as we discuss our mystical experiences with one another and the effects these have on our lives. These experiences can motivate us to quiet our minds each day and go into that peaceful place that always abides in our hearts.

When we discipline our minds, we can start the day being clear that our goal is inner peace. As we get away from the business of the world, we are then reminded that all the boundless love, peace, and spiritual fulfillment we once sought in our outside world has always been within.

As we remind ourselves of who and what we really are and what our purpose is, we then can feel more in tune and in harmony with the universe by extending our unconditional love and forgiveness to all our relationships. With every unhealed relationship that becomes healed, more light and peace come to the world. The awareness of our Oneness becomes more apparent as the illusions of separation begin to disappear. To experience Love as our only reality, all we need do is constantly give it away and be thankful for the gift of Love that has been bestowed on us by our Creator.

— GERALD G. JAMPOLSKY, M.D.
Founder and Consultant
Center for Attitudinal Healing
Sausalito, California

Foreword

Oᴜʀ ʀᴇʟᴀᴛɪᴏɴsʜɪᴘ ᴡɪᴛʜ Gᴏᴅ is our relationship with ourselves because the divine in us is who we essentially are. The idea that we are separate from God is merely an illusion of consciousness.

But that illusion is powerful indeed, and we are lost within it. The human condition is one in which we have a gnawing sense we come from somewhere else, somewhere other than this world. Yet we can't quite remember where.

Books such as this one are maps back home. They bridge us back to the essential self. They remind us who we are, and grant us the peace of remembering at last.

Without a conscious connection to love, life is beset with fear. This book is a book about a loving God, and the casting out of fear that occurs when we embrace Him. As we read the words of fellow pilgrims, particularly those who are further down the road, then our own path back home becomes illumined. We realize the part of us that says, "there is more to life than this" is not just a trick of the mind. We begin to trust we are on the right road.

The word "God" itself is a talisman, a power point, an

awesome gift. To devote ourselves to its meaning — as the pure and all-powerful love that rules the universe and lies within us all — is to merge with a divine beloved and experience a larger self. That is the goal of the spiritual seeker, and the only hope for the salvation of the world.

We are living at a time of tremendous transformation, from a species arrogant enough to think it's on its own, to a species that remembers where it comes from. When a critical mass remembers, allowing the love of the Father-Mother God to heal us of our painful illusions of separation, we will be redeemed and our children will be secure. What a task lies before us, what a gift is offered. This book is one of the many ways the spirit of love has arrived to speak with us, to beckon us and guide us home. Let us give thanks, and let us listen.

— MARIANNE WILLIAMSON
Author of *A Return to Love*
and *A Woman's Worth*

Introduction

☙

THE MAIN PURPOSE OF THIS ANTHOLOGY is to reaffirm the common denominator of all religious teachings: an individual's personal relationship with God. To do so, we have approached some of the world's leading spiritual and psychological figures to write not about their religion, but about their personal relationship with God — their day-to-day, moment-to-moment experiences.

We have been blessed, as have many readers of this anthology, with the lifetime adventure of seeking a spiritual journey. It has led us to teachers and gurus, churches and synagogues, books to be poured over, lectures to be attended — to do, in short, what we could to learn more about God and about ourselves. We found that many of these teachers and institutions try to help individuals develop a personal relationship with God, but, despite their best intentions, the very nature of the organizations and schools can interfere with that relationship. Our intention in bringing together this labor of love is to help foster an individual's ability to realize and cultivate a personal relationship with God in his or her life.

For the Love of God was written with the premise that a

spiritual foundation is the basis on which all the elements of our lives rest. Strengthening this foundation does not necessarily derive from being more pious, dogmatic, or sacrificing, but from an intimate understanding of our connection with God in every aspect of our lives.

With this in mind, each author in this collection has created an expression of personal spiritual vision. Each has shared what it is like to have a personal relationship with God, how this relationship developed, and how it manifests in his or her life, relationships, and career. Most significantly, the authors offer their insight as to how readers may enhance their connections with a higher source.

Although some authors use the name God, others the Great Spirit or higher power, and others the Dharma, readers can clearly understand that underlying almost all of the multitude of spiritual followings, a common denominator unites what may otherwise be seen as divergent beliefs. It is at this fundamental level that this book is aimed: a unifying foundation of spirituality that unites each of us.

What a wonderful experience it has been to be associated with the authors of this collection and to discover that they are living examples of their basic teachings. The contributors gave freely of their time, their thoughts, and, in many instances, their patience. They asked for nothing in return but the opportunity to share with readers what they have discovered to be true for themselves.

We created this anthology not in an effort to put forth a particular point of view, but rather as an expression of our desire to grow as individuals and to cultivate a greater understanding and sense of beauty of the universe we live in.

A significant portion of the profits from *For the Love of God* will be donated directly to a United Nations charity. We hope it will affect many lives in a positive way.

— RICHARD CARLSON, PH.D.

— BENJAMIN SHIELD, PH.D.

.I.

The Awakening Spirit

"God is a verb."

— Buckminster Fuller

Love, Compassion, and Tolerance

by HIS HOLINESS THE DALAI LAMA

"Love, compassion, and tolerance
are necessities, not luxuries.
Without them, humanity cannot survive."

THE ESSENCE OF ALL RELIGIONS IS LOVE, compassion, and tolerance. Kindness is my true religion. No matter whether you are learned or not, whether you believe in the next life or not, whether you believe in God or Buddha or some other religion or not, in day-to-day life you must be a kind person. When you are motivated by kindness, it doesn't matter whether you are a practitioner, a lawyer, a politician, an administrator, a worker, or an engineer: whatever your profession or field, deep down you are a kind person.

Love, compassion, and tolerance are necessities, not luxuries. Without them, humanity cannot survive. If you have a particular faith or religion, that is good. But you can survive without it if you have love, compassion, and tolerance. The clear proof of a person's love of God is if that person genuinely shows love to fellow human beings.

To have strong consideration for others' happiness and welfare, we must have a special altruistic attitude in which we take upon ourselves the burden of helping others. To generate such an unusual attitude, we must have great compassion — caring about the suffering of others and wanting to do something about it. To have such a strong force of compassion, we must have a strong sense of love that, upon observing sentient beings, wishes that they have happiness — finding a pleasantness in everyone and wishing happiness for everyone, just as a mother does for her sole sweet child. To have a sense of closeness and dearness for others, use as a model a person in this lifetime who was very kind to you. Then extend this sense of gratitude to all beings.

Deep down we must have real affection for each other, a clear realization or recognition of our shared human status. At the same time, we must openly accept all ideologies and systems as a means of solving humanity's problems. One country, one nation, one ideology, one system is not sufficient. It is helpful to have a variety of different approaches on the basis of a deep feeling of the basic sameness of humanity. We can then make a joint effort to solve the problems of the whole of humankind.

Every major religion has similar ideas of love, the same goal of benefiting through spiritual practice, and the same effect of making its followers into better human beings. All religions teach moral precepts for perfecting the functions of mind, body, and speech. All teach us not to lie or steal or take others' lives, and so on. The common goal of all moral precepts laid down by the great teachers of humanity is unselfishness. Those teachers wanted to lead their followers away from the paths of negative deeds caused by ignorance and to introduce them to paths of goodness. All religions can learn from one another; their ultimate goal is to produce better human beings who will be more tolerant, more compassionate, and less selfish.

Human beings need spiritual as well as material sustenance. Without spiritual sustenance, it is difficult to get and maintain peace of mind. The purpose of religion is not to argue which one is the best. Over the past centuries, each great teaching has served humanity, so it's much better to make friends, understand each other, and make an effort to serve humanity than to criticize or argue. Buddha, Jesus Christ, and all other great teachers created their ideas and teachings with sincere motivation, love, and kindness toward humanity, and they shared it for the benefit of humanity. I do not think those great teachers created differences to make trouble. Our human mind always likes different approaches. There is a richness in the fact that there are so many different presentations of the way.

There are two ways to enter into Buddhism: one through faith and one through reasoning. Faith alone may not be sufficient. Buddha always emphasized a balance of wisdom and compassion: a good brain and a good heart should work together. Placing importance on just the intellect and ignoring the heart can create more problems and more suffering in the world. On the other hand, if we emphasize only the heart, and ignore the brain, then there is not much difference between humans and animals. These two must be developed in balance, and when they are, the result is material progress accompanied by good spiritual development. Heart and mind working in harmony will yield a truly peaceful and friendly human family.

I feel that my mission is, wherever I am, to express my feeling about the importance of kindness, compassion, and the true sense of brotherhood. I practice these things. It gives me more happiness, more success. If I practice anger or jealousy or bitterness, no doubt my smile would disappear.

The real troublemakers are anger, jealousy, impatience, and hatred. With them, problems cannot be solved. Though we may have temporary success, ultimately our hatred or anger will create further difficulties. Anger makes for swift solutions. Yet, when we face problems with compassion, sincerity, and good motivation, our solutions may take longer, but ultimately they are better.

When I meet new people, in my mind there is no barrier, no curtain. As human beings you are my brothers and sisters; there is no difference in substance. I can talk with you as I would to old friends. With this feeling we can communicate without any difficulty and can make heart-to-heart contact. Based on such genuine human relations — real feeling for each other, understanding each other — we can develop mutual trust and respect. From that, we can share other people's suffering and build harmony in human society.

Creation Spirituality

by MATTHEW FOX, PH.D.

"When I'm operating at my best, my work is my prayer. It comes out of the same place that prayer comes out of — the center, the heart."

MY RELATIONSHIP WITH GOD STARTED when I was a child. I was raised in a practicing Roman Catholic home, with my parents and six brothers and sisters. When I was twelve, I had polio and lost my ability to walk. I was in the hospital for many months, and people didn't think I would ever walk again. My adolescent desire was to play football. I had to let go of that as well as much of everyday living. Children tend to face death (and letting go) more directly than adults do. Consequently, it was a great maturing experience for me.

When I regained the use of my legs and was able to do things like play football, I was overwhelmed with gratitude for something that I had previously taken for granted — my ability to walk. From that time on, gratitude has been at the heart of my spirituality. It has to do with awe — the awe of having legs, or anything else that works, the awe of just being here.

That was when I started thinking of becoming a priest. Many things affected this decision. There were the wonderful Wisconsin lakes and fields and woods where I would pray. There was the Catholic Mass, especially the Saturday masses, when priests read the wisdom literature from the Hebrew Bible. Those texts are, in effect, feminist and cosmological readings about the Mother Goddess. They spoke to my soul; they brought me, as a male, the feminine dimension of divinity, which nothing else in the 1950s culture was doing.

Then there was music. I heard Beethoven for the first time when I was in high school, and it made my soul leap. And there was literature — the works of Shakespeare and, above all, Tolstoy's *War and Peace*.

My experience with prayer is both mystical and prophetic. The mystical aspect is the falling in love with life. The prophetic aspect is the standing up to the crucifixion of Divinity, which happens every time there is injustice. That combination of pleasure (mysticism) and struggle (the prophetic) is the dialectic that creates my spirituality and my experiences with God.

There are many paths to God. Four in particular correspond to what I name in my theology "The Four Paths of Creation Spirituality." Divinity is present for me in all four paths.

The first path is the Via Positiva, or the experience of

divinity as the blessing of creation. It's what Meister Eckhart, the thirteenth-century theologian, called "is-ness." I
can pick up a blade of grass and experience its twenty-
billion-year history and its color, shape, and form. Artists
can do this: They draw a blade of grass and capture its
divinity. We can feel awe when we experience the planet,
or a dog, or a friend. Anything that has "being" is holy.
God dwells there and speaks as revelation.

This experience of divinity is a very simple thing. It's
omnipresent. The problem is our consciousness: We
need to simplify our consciousness to experience this
omnipresence of divine awe in all things, to return home.

The second path, the Via Negativa, is that of darkness, of emptiness, of nothingness, of absence. This is a
very important experience — when we suffer or experience the suffering of others, when we doubt or let go. In
the process of letting go, there is always a sinking; and in
sinking we never know when we're going to bottom out.
But as Jesus said, "I am the Way"; the way of sinking is
itself a divine experience. It takes a lot of trust. The darkness is also a kind of revelation of divinity, but it can't be
put into words. Ultimately, it's silence. With that silence
comes a union with God.

The third path is called the Via Creativa, or the Creative Way. This is an explosion. Eckhart invented the
word "breakthrough" to describe it. This is when we bottom out, when out of the darkness or through the dark
tunnel comes the light. From the story of Jesus' crucifixion (the Via Negativa) comes Easter Sunday Resurrection
(the Via Creativa). The stone is rolled away, the tomb is

opened. In the sinking process we've been so stripped and emptied that we're ready for something new. Path three is this newness — this creativity.

For myself as a writer — and for any artist in the process of creating — I realize sometimes that I am just an instrument, a channel, a conduit for a spirit far greater than myself. There's something truthful coming through me, partly because I've been so emptied by the Via Negativa that I'm not sitting around controlling things anymore. The Via Creativa is an immense experience of divinity for people. We all have it because we're all creative at some level of our being. This is the experience of co-creation. We realize, "My God, we're creating with God and God needs us to create."

The fourth path is the Via Transformativa, the Transformative Way. This path carries the imagination — this creativity, this new bliss, this new resurrection power — into society. This is the work of the prophet: to disturb the peace by sharing the good news, what Thomas Aquinas called "sharing the fruits of our contemplation." But not everyone is eager to hear the fruits of our contemplation, because people are content to live in the existing structures, psychic and social, of our society.

This is the path of struggle, the path of compassion, and the path of celebration. And the God of Celebration ritualizes with people, gets them to enjoy life again, to see life again as a child — to see the wonder, the awe, the marvel, the simplicity of the blade of grass.

Path four is also about standing up to structures that are oppressing us psychically or socially. The movements of Gandhi or King or the Nicaraguan revolution, for example, are works of the artist's path carried into the social sphere.

How can you cultivate an intimate relationship with God? If I were giving advice, first I would question: What poets do you read? What music moves you? What social issues arouse your passion? What work do you most love doing? Eckhart said, "True work is about enchantments." When does enchantment strike you? When do you feel a connection to the Universe? Where is your bliss? And what about the darkness — what have you tasted of noth- ingness? What have you tasted of the God of the dark?

In addition, I would respect your experiences. Some people come out of very wounded backgrounds. Being an uncared-for child, for example, determines much of a person's experience of God and the world.

I would encourage you to draw, to use your right brain. I often ask people to draw a picture of their expe- riences with God when they were 10, when they were 20, 30. Then I ask them to reflect on the relationship among the three experiences, how their image of God changed. Many adults, sad to say, still use the image they had when they were eight years old. In other words, their spiritual- ity has not matured. But it's there in promise, in potency. I would work at an image level instead of using just words.

I have a little trouble with the phrase "personal rela- tionship with God," because we have so psychologized reality in our culture. The "personal" tends to imply a kind of tête-à-tête, or a talking to God; a kind of projec- tion of a two-legged person, an anthropomorphizing of divinity that I think is dangerous. We need to listen as well as to talk — to listen to the glory and the pain of our times. I think that most people's basic experiences of God are like Einstein's — the awe of the universe, the experience of the cosmos as our home, and God dwelling there. Rather than say "personal relationship with God," I'd prefer to use the term "personal cosmology" — a relationship to the divine presence that dwells in us. "We dwell in God and God dwells in us." By "we," I don't mean just two-legged creatures, but the whole universe, all creatures. We must learn to be entranced again by the presence of God in all things.

I think there's danger in the "personal," for the American psyche especially. It has something to do with being stuck in our adolescence, when friendship — Am I liked? — meant everything. This idea can be projected into religion, as in "Jesus loves me." This is not adult mysticism. For one thing, it is not *child-like* enough. Children are citizens playing in the universe. True mystical adults recover that child inside and play in that personalized universe, but don't create out of God some kind of partner or mate who is missing in their lives.

When I'm operating at my best, my work is my prayer. It comes out of the same place that prayer comes out of — the center, the heart. All work is meant to be heart work: it comes out of our heart and goes to the heart. All authentic work is an effort to move other people's hearts. And this can range from music to authentic and healthy religion to decent commerce to creating objects that human beings need. Work is the way adults return the blessing of being here to the next generation. Work is relationship. And other relationships, such as friendship and mutuality and community and intimacy, I hope also come out of the same center.

How do we get in touch with that center? Through paths one, two, and three, especially at that node between paths two and three. Between the emptying of the darkness and the creativity there's a silent stillpoint that we experience as our center, through which light and grace pour. And they pour into all our relationships.

One way I pray is with Native American prayers. It's one of the most grounding and the most radical of all forms of prayer I've used. It has been the way of praying for thousands of years, and we ought to avail ourselves of such wisdom. I do a Native American sweat, and when I leave I always say *A Ho Mitakye Oyacin*, which means "to all my relations."

Native Americans constantly celebrate all their relations, which means relations to the earth, to the rocks, to the birds, the trees, the clouds, to all people of all races and all religions, and, of course, to divinity and to the spirits. But in our anthropocentric culture we hear the word "relation" and tend to think of relatives or lovers or other relationships with two-legged creatures; but the true mystical tradition says that our relations come out of the womb that birthed us all: the cosmic womb of God. We can return to this womb in the Via Negativa, which is what happens in a sweat lodge; people come out of this experience of darkness and emptiness into creativity.

To experience a personal cosmology, become a child

again — not an adolescent, but a child — and thereby become a player, a playful being in the universe. Believe, as all great teachers have told us to believe, that the universe is friendly; the universe is blessing us constantly. Become unself-conscious (Eckhart defined mysticism as unself-consciousness). If we can learn to delight again and to play again, then we will learn wisdom again. That's how we accompany God through our journey and through this universe.

The Long Journey Home:
Reconnecting with the Great Mother

by RIANE EISLER

❦

"What we think of as 'sacred' actually
is present in everything we do."

I USED TO THINK OF THE DIVINE AS "GOD." Now, if I think in
terms of a personalized deity at all, I think more of the
Goddess than of the God. I feel very strongly that our society's denial of the feminine aspect of the deity, the Mother
aspect, is one of the great obstacles to having that personal relationship, that direct connection with the divine.

I think of our whole life, from the time we're born, as
a spiritual journey in search of the experience of oneness
with the divine. There's been so much confusion about
this journey. I thought the spiritual journey meant that
you detach yourself from life, like the so-called wise men
sitting on a mountain. Now I wonder, how wise can you be
if you wrench yourself away from the human connection?

In the name of religion we have detoured from the

"partnership core" of our spirituality so terribly often. Why? This question was a major motivation for my research into prehistoric Goddess-based partnership societies. To answer it, I had to look at the whole of our history (including our prehistory) and at the whole of humanity. What emerged was a picture that affirms our spirituality and explains this detour. What I found was that, as a species, we have an innate potential for creativity, for caring, for awareness, for empathy.

My path began in childhood. I was born into a Viennese Jewish family, and when the Nazis took over we fled to Cuba. There my parents kept up Jewish traditions. Praying with my family gave me some of my most precious childhood memories. My mother baked bread for the Shabbat (Sabbath), and every Shabbat she lit the holiday candles. Have you ever seen a woman in the Jewish religion pray over the candles? She moves her hands in a beautiful, circular motion. That movement of benediction must have been part of an ancient ritual that women, as priestesses, performed long before God became only male and before only men could become priests.

I also loved praying with my father to the Jewish God. Every evening we said the "Shemah Israel" prayer in Hebrew, directed to "the Lord our God, King of the Universe." I had no clue what the Hebrew words meant, then — and now, with some sadness, I must acknowledge the disempowerment inherent in those prayers. And yet they were magical because there was so much love between my father and me. When we prayed, we shared that spiritual moment.

As a child I had a strange religious background. In Vienna I was a Jew, but in an "assimilated" Jewish family so that our religion was only a supplement to our lives. In Cuba I was a Jew living in a Catholic country attending a Methodist school. Like everyone else I had to attend chapel. So my father hired a rabbi to teach me that I was Jewish.

I was immensely drawn to the Virgin Mary, which upset my parents and was a great embarrassment to me as a Jewish child. Now I understand that it was because she was the only remnant of the Great Goddess, the mother who gives life to all of us, including the male divinity. She was still the mother of God, wasn't she?

When the war ended I was fourteen. I saw the news-reels of what had happened in the concentration camps. The God of my childhood died then, a very painful death — not for God, but for me. I had a lot of emotion invested in the relationship because I associated rituals with God. Now I understand that the role of the woman in lighting the candles and baking the bread as sacred acts of light-giving and life-nurturing was preserved and honored from when we were still empowered as priest-esses and as women to partake directly in the divine, without a male intermediary.

I didn't understand any of this at the time, only that the old familiar ideas I had been taught about what we call religion didn't make sense anymore. So I began a solitary spiritual journey. Often it was painful, because I felt I had no connection. And yet, I had.

I realized that I didn't have to go to synagogue or

church to take this journey. Gradually, I tried different things — meditation, fasting. I began to understand that we are all both the center of the universe and its most insignificant part. I began to feel that I could establish a direct connection, through my own experiences, with this large and totally mysterious reality out there that we'll never really understand with our reason, our brains. But we can know it in a different region of our selves.

Slowly, I also began to understand how, as a woman, I was in a miserable situation if I only have a God who's a Father, a King, a Lord. It implies that the only relationship I can have with the male deity is indirect. If we as women are to access the divine in us, then a female deity, a divine Mother, is essential.

For the last five thousand years, society has been oriented primarily toward what I call a dominator model. Because so much of our connection with divinity came through a hierarchy, its institutions and superimpositions interfered with our ability to have a personal relationship with the divine. This religious hierarchy stays in power by disempowering us. Presumably, we cannot have relationship with the deity without somebody (a man) who claims that only he has a real relationship with God and that we can have a relationship only according to his orders.

Through my research in archaeology, myth, and art history, I began to see that it wasn't always this way. Knowledge of the inherent spirituality of life and of nature came to us very early in our cultural evolution, as early as ten thousand years ago in the Neolithic period, with the first agrarian societies. It's revealed through the temple models unearthed by UCLA archaeologist Marija Gimbutas, where we see what she calls the "civilization of Old Europe" was a more partnership-oriented society that worshiped the Great Goddess.

In those temple models, and in other archaeological remains, we see that the traditional "women's work" was considered sacred. The temples had pottery kilns and looms for weaving cloth, mortars for grinding wheat and ovens for baking bread, because these were sacred acts. Prehistoric societies saw the living world — the heavens, the earth, everything — as a Great Mother. But though they worshiped the Great Goddess, those societies weren't matriarchies. She had both divine daughters and divine sons.

I began to see how in prehistoric societies it was much easier to be connected directly to the divine. Everything was divine, including nature. The Goddess gave life, and at death life returned to her womb, like the cycles of vegetation, to be reborn. They didn't have our current artificial distinction between spirituality and nature, with man and the spiritual seen as above woman and nature in the hierarchy.

As I continued my research I also continued my spiritual journey, and I began to see that the human spiritual impulse does not require an intermediary at all, but is inherent in the human condition. It's an evolutionary given, and its first expression was a direct way of feeling connection with the world. When we shifted from the earlier partnership model to the dominator model, we lost our sense of connection.

I believe that the denial of our connection with the Mother aspect, the feminine aspect of the deity, is one of the major obstacles to achieving that meaningful and fulfilling personal relationship not only with the deity but with one another. We all can observe the element of the feminine, of the Mother, of the nurturer, from our experiences of a mother. The Great Mother also has a dark aspect, however: the transformative aspect of reclaiming life at death. But to have been deprived of that motherly dimension in the deity reflects something in our dominator society: a deadening of empathy, a deadening of caring, a denial of the feminine in men, and a contempt for women and the feminine.

It's not accidental that today there's so much interest in spirituality. We're trying to reconnect. Even though many of us don't think of spirituality in the context of social systems, we are beginning to recognize that the conquest mentality and the idea of a male God with men made in His image who dominate over women, children, and the rest of nature could be the swan song for us as a species.

When the dominator model no longer obstructs our search, we can begin the real spiritual journey. The task of clearing the obstacles is to get the point when we can explore our relationship to the divine. The more we move toward a partnership model of society, the more we can search for our higher potential. Humans have the capacity for creativity, for love, for justice, for searching for wisdom and beauty. All these are paths to the divine.

Of all the knowledge that we're reclaiming about

prehistoric societies, one of the most touching is the knowledge of the sacral in everyday life — the understanding that what we think of as "sacred" actually is present in everything we do. We can build a society where all of life is imbued with that connectedness, of the extraordinary miracle of life, of the beauty and mystery and sometimes tragedy of nature and of ourselves as part of nature.

Today's society calls for an unraveling process and then a reweaving. But we don't need to throw out the baby with the bathwater. For example, many Jewish and Christian teachings contain a partnership core: a core of caring, respect. I want to keep that. Real love is empathic — an act of service. We must manifest the love of God in action as well as in thought and word. We need greater understanding, but we also need the sacred acts: the sacred act of giving birth, the sacred act of making bread and of sharing that bread. These are all ritual acts in the sense of ritual as an act of love, not as an act of suffering.

Women are taught in patriarchal cultures that they're supposed to serve. But it's not enough to honor and to serve others. We also must honor and serve ourselves. We must nurture ourselves. If we become victims and martyrs, we are not serving anyone, because we deny our own divinity. We don't honor ourselves, our own worth. There is a fine line between serving so that we maintain respect for ourselves and our dignity and serving so that we grovel and lose our dignity. The institutionalized religions, by and large, have not given us that balanced view, and we need to find it. Some milestones of my spiritual journey include knowing, and reclaiming, the long-ago traditions when the sacred and the divine had a female form, and knowing that I am not cut off from them because I happen to be a woman.

In tangible, concrete ways I redefined my understanding of what I mean by deity, by ritual, by sacred, by love. I now understand why, for example, I feel so connected with the divine when I see beauty, when I look at a sunset. I understand that the artificial distinction between the spiritual and the natural is just part of the baggage I can leave behind. I understand why I feel so good when I'm able to reach out a hand to someone. I don't do it as an artificial thing, because of a command from some remote punitive deity or some priest or pope or other man who's going to punish me if I don't. Quite the contrary: I do it because it gives me pleasure. And this pleasure is partly because such giving is innate in us.

Whom will we trust to guide our spiritual journeys? Do we trust what somebody else — an authority, a priest, whether Christian, Muslim, Buddhist, whatever — tells us? Or do we trust our own connection to the deity? How can we really own that relationship, internalize it, empower ourselves, and become part of the creative and healing power in the universe?

Beware of advice about how to find the deity. Follow your own path.

The Secret in the Center

by Wayne Dyer, Ph.D.

꩜

"In a realistic, here-and-now sense, my daily,
moment-to-moment experience of God is to love
and to serve and to give."

While my family and I were visiting the island of
Maui, in Hawaii, my relationship to God under-
went a dramatic change — almost an explosion of spirituality.

One night my wife and I had gone to sleep without
resolving some differences. The next morning I was
awake at five-thirty, unusually early for me, and decided
to walk along the beach. After a while I sat down and
began to meditate. I have endorsed the practice of meditation for a long time but have done it only sporadically
throughout my adult life. While I was meditating something incredible happened, what I'd call an experience of
euphoric love, as if I were actually talking to God, as if I

were in His presence. There were spiraling lights and a kundalini yoga feeling that went up my spine, like a warm shower running inside myself. I was definitely in another level of consciousness. I came back from the walk, discussed what had happened with my wife, and soon everything was fine between us again.

I decided to do the same thing the next morning and, without setting an alarm, was again awake at five-thirty. As I began my meditation, an inner glow again came to me, similar to the day before. I heard myself talking to God and receiving messages about the nature and purpose of life. Since those initial experiences, I've done the same thing every morning and have made a commitment to do so every day for the rest of my life.

The result of those powerful experiences was that I have redirected my life to assess all my behavior, my thinking, and my actions in terms of whether I am able to love, give, or serve. If I'm not doing one of these, then I'm not in harmony with the messages I received.

I spent the first ten years or so of my life in a series of homes, including a Methodist foster home and a Baptist orphanage. I experienced a tremendous amount of orthodoxy and a great deal of fear. Church was not a very pleasant place for me. The God of one church was a frightening thing, with devils and Holy Ghosts. I used to joke that if someone holds you under water long enough (as in baptism), eventually you'll come around to that point of view.

As I grew older, I tended to stay away from most "religious experiences." I thought, Yes, there's something there, but I really don't know much about it, and I was too busy pursuing other things. But over the last fifteen years my emphasis and path have shifted toward the spiritual. That magnificent experience in Hawaii showed me there is a powerful world beyond what we usually see — a world of thought, spirit, higher consciousness — a world of God that is within all form.

In every age and civilization, three ideas about life and beyond seem to overlap. The first is that there's an infinite, invisible world beyond the world that we experience. The second is that this infinite world is a part of every human personality. And the third is that the purpose of life is to discover this infinite world.

Some call this infinite world God. Others call it Krishna, Spirit, Higher Consciousness, Buddha, or Christ. I think it's important not to get bogged down in the labels. They cannot describe that which is infinite. After all, you can't drink the word "water" or float a ship in the formula H_2O. You can only experience water. Thoreau said, "Your religion is where your love is." Instead of being concerned with whether I'm a Christian or a Jew or a Buddhist, I try to think of myself as striving to be Christ-like or Buddha-like. I prefer to see these spiritual masters as offering us incredible role models of loving and serving and giving to each other and to the world.

You can't use the world of form to get to the world that is beyond form. You have to use another standard. If you weighed a dying person, watched as life left, and then weighed the body that just housed life, it would weigh the same. What can't be weighed is what constituted the life, the humanity, the very essence. After life passed out of a body, that body is revealed as only a package that housed the person.

I look at my own form and see hairs falling out where I want them and growing in places where I don't want them, and skin hanging less tightly on the bones. If I thought that this was all I am, I would see myself as a bag of bones who's shriveling up and withering away to an abyss of nothingness. But when I experience God, I know I'm only *occupying* this present form. We really are ageless and timeless, beyond cause and effect, beyond beginnings and endings, beyond form and all the rules that apply to form.

Coming into contact with the formless part of our humanity is what I mean by coming into contact with God. I know that I am a spiritual being having a temporary human experience. I now attempt to connect to all the people in my life in terms of meeting not their form — what I call their "package" — but rather the divine part that is beyond their form. When we discover this beautiful part of human beings, we begin to see an enormous harmony in life; we begin to discover the connectedness of everyone and everything. In a realistic, here-and-now sense, my daily, moment-to-moment experience of God is to love and to serve and to give. To do so, I must have ease within myself and cooperate with the living cells adjacent to me and the living cells adjacent to humanity. My body is alive with millions of life forms, yet they all have a reference to the whole; they all work in harmony and constitute my being.

Everything that happens outside us has its counter-part within us, and vice versa. I am both one being composed of millions of life forms (all of which must be in harmony for me to function) and also one cell in the total body called humanity. If any cell in the total body called humanity has disease within it, then it will not cooperate with the cell adjacent to it. It has no reference to the whole. So a cancer in my body and a cancer in society are essentially identical. These cells have no reference to the whole, and they're gobbling everything in their wake until they destroy the whole and themselves.

The only way the world will be transformed is for the world's inhabitants to make changes in individual levels of consciousness. As we do this, we experience God. God becomes that harmony. Robert Frost said it beautifully: "We all sit around in a circle and suppose, but the secret sits in the center and knows." That center is where I now go when I meditate. I go into that light and I also bring it to me. Like an axle that turns but whose center doesn't move, God is the unmoved secret in the center.

All the Eastern traditions talk about having an inner observer, being able to "die" while you're alive. To be spiritual, to awaken, to be detached means to experience your own death. What does it mean to die while you're alive? It means coming into contact with the part of you that doesn't constitute your humanity. The invisible part of you — the part of you that leaves when you die — is where God resides. And this isn't "mystical"; it's real. You don't have to go to India to discover it; you don't have to wear a loincloth and meditate in a cave.

I find God by giving myself time every day — through prayer, or meditation, or whatever you want to call it — to go into another level of consciousness. I close my eyes and breathe. I center myself and empty my mind and begin to feel the love that is there when I quiet down enough to feel. As I do this I transcend time and space, and I am in the very presence of God. This, to me, is a direct daily experience of God, and it puts me into a state of harmony and bliss that transcends anything I've ever known.

Now, I experience the love in everyone. I no longer am a person who judges others for being overweight, for being too young or too old, for having their hair a certain way, or for how they dress. When you judge others, you don't define them, you define yourself as someone who needs to judge and compartmentalize people. My experience with God is that I no longer have to define myself as someone who does that. My goal is to experience unconditional love and acceptance and joy for everyone, even those who are behaving in ways that I find difficult to accept.

The highest spiritual act in life is to see yourself in everyone else and everyone else in you, to surrender yourself and see everyone's joy and suffering as your own, to detach yourself from your ego-need to be attached to the fruits of your labor, and to simply see everyone else in the world as part of you. Gandhi was asked to describe in twenty-five words or less what his life mission was. He said, "I could do it in three: 'Renounce and enjoy.'" You renounce all worldly attachment to everything and enjoy what God gives you. You give away what you have inside yourself, your love. You're not concerned with whether it worked or didn't work, whether it was right or wrong, whether you won or lost. You just constantly flow through your life without getting attached to the results. The irony is that the less attached you are, the more you get. The more you keep circulating, the more keeps coming back to you. It's a flowing system.

Many people are too left-brain, too linear, too impatient to give themselves the time to tap into God. Cultivating a personal relationship with God means giving yourself the daily opportunity to be in that place where all your thoughts are connected to the higher intelligence that's in all form. How you do it doesn't matter. It doesn't come about in some linear fashion or by studying somebody else's ways. The secret is in giving yourself permission to experience it firsthand and then living whatever messages you're getting. When you experience this, you connect in a loving way to everything in the universe.

.II.

❧

The
God
Within

*"You are the content of your consciousness;
in knowing yourself you will know the universe."*

— J. Krishnamurti

Grace, Gratitude, and the Sacred Experiences

by JEAN SHINODA BOLEN, M.D.

*"My deep sense of spiritual meaning has to do with
remembering as much as it has to do with discovering."*

I MOVE THROUGH MY DAY-TO-DAY LIFE with a sense of
appreciation and gratitude that comes from knowing
how fortunate I truly am and how unearned all that I am
thankful for really is. To have this perspective in my everyday consciousness is in itself a gift, for it leads to feeling
"graced," or blessed, each time. For example, my workday
commute takes me through a tunnel toward the Golden
Gate Bridge. Sometime I emerge to see a panoramic view
of bay and bridges and city, or perhaps I see only the tops
of the bridge towers emerging through the thick fog. I
am struck by how beautiful each sight is. Every time I see
beauty around me I appreciate what I am seeing, and
simultaneously I have this sense of appreciation — for
being alive to have this particular moment.

My children evoke a much deeper sense of gratitude. Feelings mixed with simultaneous appreciation well up in me toward them. There is a sensation in the middle of my chest, and the words that I stopped saying out loud, "You warm the cockles of my heart," come to mind. I have never taken my children for granted or have been unaware that things could have been different. That they were preceded by three miscarriages is only part of it. The miracle of new life that I felt when they were born left an indelible mark on my psyche. I remember being awed, recalling the perfection of a little hand with nails perfectly formed in miniature and the stillpoint numinous experiences of nursing or holding them during the middle of the night.

In my work, when I am able to make a difference to someone, catch a glimpse of a person's soul, or hear a dream and sense how profound the human psyche is, I feel privileged to be in this moment. And when I narrowly escape being in an accident or have some sense of a close call, I literally and physically appreciate being alive and unharmed in this moment. When I feel this gratitude-for-being, it is like singing a thank-you and hearing a response in which divinity is present.

When San Francisco suffered an earthquake in which most were spared and the potential for devastation averted, it seemed as if our entire community responded from the heart with thankfulness and helpfulness. People commented on how wonderful this was, how what really matters became clear, and why did we have to have a disaster for us to realize this? For a time, what we had, compared to what could have been taken away, was in our consciousness, and we felt gratitude.

As I was growing up, I became very much aware that bad things happen to people; medical school, internship, and residency further brought this home to me, case by case. My work as a psychiatrist has added to this awareness. I do not know that there is an answer to the question, "why them and not me?" As a consequence, however, of witnessing the suffering and abuse that has happened to others, when bad things happen to me I do know that this, too, is part of my life: my turn to experience pain and loss, which is partly redeemed by my conviction that no experience goes to waste. As a therapist and teacher, through my writing or analytic work, whatever happens to me will help me someday to better understand and help someone.

Over the years I have come to believe that life is full of unchosen circumstances, that being human has to do with the evolution of our individual consciousness and with it, responsibilities for choice. Pain and joy both come with life. I believe that how we respond to what happens to us and around us shapes who we become and has to do with the psyche or the soul's growth. Now that I am in my fifth decade, I can look back and say that the hardest and darkest times in my life led me deeper and farther along my spiritual path. At the same time I am not at all sure that, at least in this life, such is the case for everyone, especially the very young who are abused or who arrive in this world innately handicapped.

It has not been the difficult times, however, that most

shaped my spiritual life, but the times that were "sacramental" — situations that were imbued with grace, sacred moments in which I felt the presence of God or Goddess or felt connected to the universe or Tao. Or those times I was in nature or at a sacred site, and felt myself enter a sacred place, or have a sacred meeting, a soul-to-soul communion with another person. These are the experiences that have really mattered, the ones that changed me — the spiritual experiences that led me to what I am doing with my life. I directly felt the presence of divinity, and knew it. Each experience was subjectively and intensely real, more so than ordinary reality.

When I was sixteen, I was literally brought to my knees, humbled by a religious experience that made me aware of how fortunate I was and how prideful I had been for accomplishments and abilities that were gifts. I felt the grace of God in a transcendent movement, which put my life in perspective and moved me to pray and to mean, "Thy will, not mine, be done." In that experience of humility and grace and submission, I became convinced that I should become a doctor to serve others who were less fortunate. There is absolutely no way I would have taken that path (given my decided lack of ability and enthusiasm for science and math), except for that experience. And over the years, in less intense ways, I've received more lessons in humility, invariably after feeling superior or subtly arrogant. Humility has been a source of wisdom and learning.

In every sacred moment there is a sense of timelessness and wholeness, of having a place in the Universe, of mattering, which I have experienced as both a revelation and a confirmation of something familiar, somehow already known, even as I may experience it consciously for the first time. I believe through my subjective experience that my deep sense of spiritual meaning has to do with remembering as much as it has to do with discovering. "What it is" that I remember or discover in each experience of divinity is archetypal and ineffable, a gnosis or knowledge of inestimable value. I respond to the grace I feel with gratitude and a commitment to live by what I intuitively and experientially know to be true for me.

God Lost and Regained

by HOWARD MURPHET

❧

*"When we come to know our inner God, which is our
true Self, we will know that the divine is in everybody."*

I CANNOT REMEMBER A TIME IN MY CHILDHOOD when I did
not know of the existence of God. But my image of God
now is not my image of God then. My mother, who was my
first spiritual teacher, taught me that God was a great
being who lived in the heavens. From there, He saw
everything that happened on earth, including what I
thought and did and said. One morning on our farm,
when I was about five, I went to gather eggs. I found five,
but on the way back to the house I dropped one and it
broke. I decided I would tell my mother that there were
only four eggs. But then I remembered the eye of God
from above — He certainly knew there had been five, and
if I told a lie, His punishment might be much greater
than anything my mother would inflict on me.

Yet this God, I was taught, was also an omnipotent and wise God. If I prayed to Him — which I did every morning and evening — then He could answer my prayers and give me anything I asked for as long as it was good for me. He had wisdom to know what was best. Although I didn't understand why his son Jesus Christ had died for all humanity, I accepted it and felt a great deal of love for him.

In secondary school, studying science and mathematics awakened new areas of reasoning and brought me into a new, rational world. I began to doubt, but I did not discard the God of my childhood. In my last year of grammar school, I decided to be a minister. Like many young people in their teens, I had a desire to spend my life doing good for humanity. However, before the year was out, I definitely decided that I could not accept the dogma of the church.

The last remnants of my childhood God vanished during my academic studies at the university. My attitude was that of the agnostic. I knew that I did not know, that I would need further proof before I could again believe wholeheartedly in the existence of God. Even so, I always had a deep-down feeling that there was something, but I longed for further proof and further knowledge.

I spent some years working on newspapers. During this period my longing to regain the God I had lost sank into the background. I developed a strong desire to travel, to visit many countries and learn of men and manners, and to experience all there was to experience in the world. In this way I thought I would learn something to help answer my innermost questions about "life, death, and the vast forever." I also felt an urge to write. My ambition was to express, in books, what I could learn of the world and life and its meaning.

While waiting to begin my travels, I appeased my heart by reading poems that spoke of wanderlust. I read, with great pleasure, such things as the travels of Ulysses. I thought of myself like Ulysses, forever wandering with a hungry heart. I know now, though I was not fully aware of it then, that the hunger in my heart was for the God I had lost.

My world travels began when I sailed from Australia to England just before World War II. When the war came, I joined the Red Cross, then the British Army. The spiritual highlight of the early part of my war travels was the three months I spent in Palestine. I experienced joy in being in the country that was the setting of the Christ. In fact, Palestine seemed not so much like a real country as a stage setting for the great drama. Visiting places sacred to that drama made the Christ story seem very real in time — it seemed to belong to eternity. And so did the sandy soil where his sandals had trod. I could tell by the way I was stirred that the Christ story was deep in my bones. Nevertheless, this experience did not revive the God of my childhood.

After the war, through a series of events, my wife and I arrived in India, at the headquarters of the Theosophical Society. For several years we studied the ancient wisdom of the Far East and India, with emphasis on the Hindu spiritual philosophy. This new world of understanding took me far beyond the limitations of modern science, which is, as one great scientist said, "like picking up a pebble on the beach, while all the great ocean of the unknown lies beyond you." Theosophical teachings affirm an unknowable principle beyond the universe, called Brahman by the Indians and, by some Western philosophers, the Absolute. From this eternal, divine principle the whole cosmos emanates.

Theosophy elevated my mind and broadened my horizons, but it still left my heart empty. It did not replace the homey, loving, fatherly God of my childhood. So my heart remained hungry for something more.

It seems that when the yearning for spiritual nourishment is strong enough, the Divine One takes a hand. And so I was led to the spiritual teacher Satya Sai Baba. In my first interview with him, in his ashram, I was taken to an inner room where he gave me a baptism of divine love. It was like a holy warm oil pouring through and soaking every atom of my physical body. This experience brought about a major inner change.

But this transformation was not immediate. Baba had shattered the shell of my arid heart, and the broken pieces took some time to clear away. Gradually, I was led to a new set of values in life and to a new understanding of life's meaning, purpose, and destiny. The God I had lost through the higher education of my mind returned to me in an expanded form, one that satisfied the critical intellect that had floundered away. Through Baba's teaching, I came to understand that the divine is formless and, as a formless spirit, occupies every space of matter and is in the whole of the universe. But in addition, there is also God with form. God can take any form and, in fact, does. When His presence on earth is essential for saving humanity from destroying itself, He comes to earth in the form of a human. He has done this many times in our history.

In the broadest sense, we could say that God has taken all the forms that exist in the universe and is, indeed, in all of them. When we come to know our inner God, which is our true Self, we will know that the divine is in everybody, so there is a great feeling of unity with all life, which expresses itself in the form of divine love. That divine love must embrace everything — not only people we like but also people we do not like. I began to think of the people whom I regarded as my enemies, and I took them into my heart and mind to forgive them all and to bring them into the circle of my feeling of love for all.

There are so many wrong ideas to be cast aside; so many overpowering desires to be brought under control, to be reigned in like wild horses and steered in the right direction; so many egotistical emotions to be controlled. We prodigal sons returning to our Father's home and our spiritual home will meet with many snares and illusions along the way. But Sai Baba said, "It is possible to reach home in this lifetime, and we are in fact here in a body in order to do just that — to wake up to a divine identity and hurry back towards our homes." It may take more than one lifetime, perhaps many lifetimes after we have realized the purpose of our lives. But however long it takes, the result is certain. Every human soul will return to the Godhead from where it started and, in returning to where it began, will, in the words of T.S. Eliot, "know the place for the first time."

Avatar Sai Baba has proven for me beyond question that God has those three basic qualities my mother taught me: omnipresence, omniscience, and omnipotence. It stands to reason that He is omnipresent because, as in the formless divine principle or spirit, He is everywhere within everything. There is no part of space that He does not fill. This is an all-knowing conscious spirit. Yet, because Sai Baba, in the form of a man, is not everywhere, how can he know everything? Well, it seems to my limited understanding that he is able to "plug in" to his own formless self, and when it is of value to his mission, he is able to be where he wishes to be and to know what is being said and done and thought. One day my wife and I were talking about our plans to leave the ashram, return to the headquarters of the Theosophical Society, and rent a flat near a library where I could quietly work on my book. We did not really want to leave Baba, but felt that moving away for a few months was the correct thing to do. A few days later we were with Sai Baba, and he said suddenly, "Yes, I think it's a good idea that you should go and spend some time away to do your work"!

Sai Baba has demonstrated to me his power to help people in their difficult days, wherever they may be. Seeing these miracles led me, at last, to believe fully in the miracles of Jesus Christ. Baba led me to a deeper understanding and appreciation of many aspects of Christianity. For example, he said that the death of Jesus on the cross was a symbol of the crossing out of lower ego, and that we all must in the same way allow our egos to be crucified so that our higher, true selves may rise. I find this a good, satisfactory explanation of why Jesus died for us — to show us the way.

My wife and I have been led to a new way of life through the influence and teachings of our teacher. Our values and aims in life are now different. We know why we're here and where we are going and how we should get there. Those who would come to God and this deeper understanding of the meaning of life may do so if their yearning, if their divine discontent, if their hunger for spiritual sustenance is strong enough. Then there is no doubt they will be led to the right guide.

And the highest and most glorious destination of humanity is not the lower heavens or paradises but the Godhead itself. There, we will feel and we will know that we are what we have always been — one with the divine. This high destination, this liberation from the bondage of suffering and sorrow, can be reached in this life.

What Personal Life?

by Reverend Michael Beckwith

"Gathering with other seekers creates a field of receptivity that we can all tap into. As we come together to pray and celebrate and worship — bringing the focus of our attention on God, good, love, service, and beauty — we delve deeper into that awareness."

WE DON'T REALLY HAVE A PERSONAL LIFE apart from God. What we call our life is actually the presence of God personified as us. The illusion of a separate life causes a tremendous amount of pain, frustration, discomfort, and disease in our life. The belief that a personal life exists apart from God creates experience disconnected from God. This is painful and frustrating. Our spiritual work is to break down the illusion that we have a life here and that a life of God is somewhere else. All of our prayer work, our meditation work, our affirmation work — the path individuals take to grow spiritually — is primarily to break down that sense of separation from God.

It's extremely important that we do the work because without an awareness of what we are, the unique pattern of God within each individual won't be expressed. Every human being, like every flower, has a unique pattern of expression. We all have a kaleidoscope of good in us — a deeper dimension accessed through our awareness that God is expressed through us and as us. So, it's not only important, it's the only game in town. It's the reason we're here.

A rose's purpose is to grow and become strong enough to bloom. When you have matured spiritually, you bloom into an awareness of your oneness with God. Without that awareness, you are immature, regardless of how much you have attained in the world materialistically, intellectually, or emotionally.

The process can be difficult. I believe the appearance that we're separate from God leads us to think that we can control our life. In truth, because our life is the life of God, It can manage itself. But we resist letting God manifest through us because some part of us wants to stay the same. Rather than change ourselves, we want to change the world and other people. But spiritual growth is just the opposite. It's about letting go of opinion, false thought, and erroneous perceptions so this other dimension can emerge. It is about totally shifting our identity. The pain comes because the ego doesn't know the difference between annihilation and transformation. So when your point of view shifts, it feels like dying. But of course you aren't dying; for the first time you are becoming fully alive.

Jesus said something I've always loved: "I have come bearing not peace but a sword to set mother at variance against her daughter, father at variance against his son ... " I've always interpreted that to mean, "I have come to cut away your lesser identities. Before you thought of yourself simply as your mother and father's child. I have come to open you to a greater identity, to bring you to understand that there is only one father, which is God."

So the lesser part of us identifies with being the son or daughter of our human heritage, but the greater part of us is eternal. Our work is to tap into that deeper dimension and learn how to let It take over, so that Its thoughts are our thoughts, Its perception is our perception, and Its perspective is our perspective. When we do this, our thoughts, words, and actions become expressions of God's love and wisdom.

Some time ago, I coauthored a song about how people are actually asleep, dreaming they're awake. I believe the average person is sleepwalking. In their dream state they try to control their world and be comfortable. Then, when they wake up, they discover that they're literally surrounded by God's presence. They're in God's grace, and God's grace is in them. They become fully alive and vitalized — and they wonder what they were doing before.

My passion for God is a deep and abiding love in the presence of God. God is everything to me. The lights went on for me well over twenty years ago, and I've never looked back. This level of passion or, as athletes would say, "staying hungry," or "being on the edge," has not diminished over the years. In fact, it's intensified. My level of commitment and discipline is even higher now than when I started. I wake up in the morning still hungry and thirsty for truth and righteousness. I'm constantly checking that I'm available for the presence of God. Being captured by a vision for your life fuels you; it gives you a passion and energy you can't get from the world.

People often ask about my meditation and prayer time. I tell them how I meditate in the morning, in the evening and throughout the day. They think, it would take a superman to do that. And I say, "No, people who *don't* practice daily are supermen. It takes a superman to be in the world, with all its powerful antispiritual influences." I've lived both ways, and I'd rather take the course of daily prayer and meditation. As I constantly recommit to God's vision, something else within me does the work. I don't have to make it through life on my own limited intelligence and power. To me, it's easier to yield to the Presence, yield to God, yield to love. I just have to get out of the way. I have to submit myself. I have to be available.

Everyone can find a personal relationship with God. It does take earnestness, discipline, and commitment. But if a person truly wants to wake up, that earnestness will yield fruit. When the scriptures say, as they do in so many different ways, that those who hunger and thirst after truth and righteousness shall be fed, I believe they're talking about how that sense of earnestness makes God real to us.

It's important to know the difference between being an aspirant and a disciple. To me, an aspirant wants the results of spiritual living without paying the price. Disciples, on the other hand, completely surrender to the earnest desire within themselves to wake up. And when people really become disciples, nothing stops them until they wake up, whether it's going to churches, synagogues, or spiritual centers; finding the right book; or seeking inspiring ideas in the media. Earnestness itself creates an atmosphere where insight will happen. Their inner voice will speak to them.

Some people choose the path of keeping themselves available to God from the beginning. Others may need it pushed on them. If they live in laziness and hope the rewards of spirituality are just going to happen, then they're enrolling in the school of pain. The prisons they create will cause anguish, which, in turn, creates the need for an earnest search. The pain will push them until their vision appears, and then the vision takes over. Even so, they have to choose to embrace the vision and leave the pain behind.

Either way, if you take your heart's earnest desire to know God, and sit down every day with that and with your favorite book, your favorite author, or your favorite tape, you will be rewarded. Your spiritual realization will become more real to you than the experience of the world. When that happens, when God becomes more real to you, you will learn to exercise the commitment and discipline to stay in God-consciousness, to keep yourself truly awake. It doesn't matter who you are: the worst criminal or the best do-gooder both have the same opportunity to create a personal relationship with the spirit of the living God.

As we grow, our perception and awareness of God changes. We may begin with an elementary view of God as an individual outside ourselves who controls us and the universe. There's an old saying that God made us in His image, and we've been trying to return the favor ever since. People often view God in a human image. This God changes His mind, gets upset, answers some prayers but not others, loves some people but not others. But even with that limited image, if we pray sincerely, we'll eventually realize that God is changeless. He's the same all the time because He's not in time — time is in Him.

Beginning seekers, especially, need to find time for God in their life, to find the discipline to make themselves available to God. If you do this at the same time every day, it will grow into a habit, and then into a way of life. When I was a beginner, I got up every morning at seven to meditate and pray; every night before I bed I meditated, prayed, and read spiritual material. Eventually, the boundaries between my practice and the rest of my life broke down. I discovered that while my official meditation and prayer time ended at eight, I was still praying. When I'd meet somebody at work, the prayer was still within me. If I was about to say something that wouldn't foster friendship or love, the prayer would quiet me. After awhile I realized that my life was the prayer. Instead of fitting meditation and prayer into my life, I built my life around celebrating the presence of God.

Now I perform formal prayers to augment my way of life. When I wake up, the first thing I do is say, "Thank you, God — for my life, my breath. Thank you for everything." I say, "Yes, I'm here for You. Yes, I'm available. Yes, I'm ready." Even if I don't feel like it emotionally or physically, I try to engage my yes. So, I may say yes out loud: "Yes. Yes to life. Yes to love. Yes to God. Yes to beauty. Yes to creativity, excellence, integrity. Yes, yes, yes, yes, yes, yes, yes, yes."

I also do physical exercise, Hatha Yoga, jogging, and light weight-training. And I formally meditate and pray. I never spend less than a half hour, but more often than not, I take an hour or more to commune with God. Then I'm into my day. I also try to do a spiritual retreat a couple of times a year where I sit in silence for three to seven days at a time.

There are many ways people experience God. Sometimes, God flows through us despite our feelings that God is separate. We sometimes feel we're not ready or worthy, so we open ourselves and God pours through us despite our foibles. In other moments, the lights are dim and we don't see as clearly. We may still intellectually know our connection with God, but God seems outside of us. Finally, in other moments we cannot tell where we begin and God ends or God's life begins and our life ends. We feel completely at one with God.

There are appropriate prayers for each level. If you feel absolutely separate from God, you may find that your prayer is one of beseeching. At another level, you may evoke a law or decree to set the flow of God in motion through you. At another point, you may feel so connected and in prayer that the *prayer* is praying *you*. You may find yourself proclaiming that God is everywhere, love is everywhere. All these prayers are appropriate.

However, prayers of beseeching generally are successful because people become so exhausted that they let go and let God in. Remember, it's essential to know that all prayer is about having a shift in perception — moving from the illusion of separation to an awareness of our Oneness with the Presence. It's about moving from three-dimensional thinking to full-dimensional awareness.

Those of us trying to live a life we are proud of still make mistakes. It's natural and human. And we have to learn how to forgive ourselves. Often, we hang onto the guilt. That's really focusing on our ego, another way of trying to control our life. We feel that God will judge us, so we say to ourselves, "I might as well do the job myself. God will see how much I'm hating myself already and will lighten up on me."

In fact, self-abuse only prevents you from opening to the grace of God that's always there. God knows and loves you completely. God is not waiting for you to get your act right before He can forgive you. The nature of God is love; knowing that will make it easier for you to return to God's grace. When you realize you made a mistake and sincerely regret it, your regret means you're willing to change your actions or your perspective so it doesn't happen again. You can embrace yourself. You become available again to God, because God is still there. You had cut off the relationship by hanging onto guilt and by thinking that God was going to punish you.

Self-forgiveness is a discipline. So often people don't feel alive unless they're experiencing emotional drama. They get caught up in feeling they are a bad person and thinking that God will punish them. At some point, as you begin to mature spiritually, it's the connection with God that lets you know you're alive.

Another important part of our spiritual journey is fellowship and group worship. Gathering with other seekers creates a field of receptivity that we can all tap into. As we come together to pray and celebrate and worship — bringing the focus of our attention on God, good, love, service, and beauty — we delve deeper into that awareness. The group energy amplifies the work.

Fellowship is very important because in our industrialized Western society, our values focus on acquiring, hoarding, greed, and competition. You begin to think that's normal because you receive recognition and status for excelling in this world. When you join with others who are trying to grow spiritually, you practice a different set of values: compassion, giving, generosity of heart, time, and support rather than competition. Joining in a group is very, very dynamic, and very important for spiritual growth.

In the materialistic world, you often drop to the lowest common denominator of the emotions, but in the spiritual community, you can often transcend your emotions. You can have an insight into reality and that changes your point of view, your emotions, and your thoughts. It's beautiful. This transcendence is why so many people in a group are carried further than they thought possible. "Wow," they say. "After the service, after we held hands, after we prayed together, I saw things differently."

Even after you've experienced the gifts of fellowship, you need to develop a strategy for staying focused and available. You must remember that your solo work is equally important. Joining a group by itself can sometimes become a form of addiction, if you're not also doing your own work. If you're riding the coattails of someone else's spiritual leadership, but you're not doing your own spiritual work, then you become a groupie rather than someone empowered by the energy of God.

To me, the key to spiritual growth and God-consciousness is understanding that we're not in the world to look for a new belief system. Instead, we're looking for ways to awaken to our real self. We are each to become the best person we can be. The quest is not about this or that religion, this or that teacher, this or that belief. It's what we can do to know who we are, and then to express our authentic spiritual identity in our human incarnation. With that perspective, we open ourselves to a greater level of empowerment and move ourselves from being victims of external forces to being expressions of God's great love and wisdom.

God is Spirit, an ineffable, all-knowing Presence that is everywhere in its fullness. Where you see words like "Him," please be aware that God is beyond gender. God is.

God as Essence

by A.H. ALMAAS

❧

*"To truly find God, truth needs to be found
independently from the opinions of others.
The truth has to be found in our hearts."*

I WAS BROUGHT UP, IN A MUSLIM COMMUNITY, with a
belief in God. There was a strong emphasis on the
teachings of God, but I remember that I could not accept
at face value what was taught to me. I felt that I needed to
find out for myself what the nature of reality was, whether
it was God, and what the true nature of God was.

At the beginning of my spiritual journey I became
aware of the experience of what I now refer to as the
"essence" of the human being. There was an arising within, experienced intimately and directly, of a living presence, a palpable feeling of a living, self-aware truth. For
many years now, this presence has revealed itself within
me as pure spiritual qualities, first the differentiated

qualities of its presence, which include truth, awareness, spaciousness, love, compassion, joy, and contentment; then its undifferentiated pure presence of Being, which revealed the various subtleties inherent in its experience, both within and beyond concepts.

Soon after the beginning of my spiritual journey, I recognized that this presence exists, and is true, for every human being; that it is the essential nature of everyone, and, hence, it is independent from any one person's history or life circumstance. Essence is something we are born with — our birthright. Essence is not something we have to work toward, for it is what we truly are. Therefore, a spiritual path is really one of removing the obstructions that disguise this essence.

This presence is a practical, day-to-day kind of experience, not something abstract or otherworldly. It has an innate intelligence that is beyond anyone's mind. At first I didn't exactly think of it as God, although I may have thought of it as the God within. Eventually, this presence revealed itself to be the inner nature of everything, and I began feeling more and more that this living consciousness, this pure essence of being, was God. I called it Truth, Reality, Being, or God.

In my experience, as I open myself to seeing the truth of who and what I am, God is a truth that reveals itself on its own. It is independent from anyone's mind or preferences, and has always existed and always will exist inside each of us. God, for me, means experiencing the totality of all existence in its true nature and condition. This means perceiving the unity of all that can be perceived, all that can be seen, at all levels of reality, including all beings and everything that appears in experience. With God, nothing is separate from anything else. By this I don't mean a scientific interconnectedness, but rather only one and single presence. This unity has perfection and beauty to it.

My experience is that we are all "one being." There is no separate individual experiencing God. This conception of God means that my experience of myself as a separate individual does not truly exist. This does not mean that I am God, but instead, I, like everyone else, am part of the presence that is alive and conscious.

God can be seen in His beingness and God can be seen in His essence. They are slightly different, although they are inseparable. Beingness means actual nature, physical actuality of existence, perceived existence of God or the God presence. This is the totality of all that exists, all the universe including my physical body, your physical body, the telephone, the room, the air, the light, the sound — all as one reality, one presence, one body that is pure consciousness, intelligence, and love. But that one reality has an essence, an inner nature. I call it the essence of God. This is the absolute mystery, the dazzling beauty that is beyond existence and nonexistence, the timeless source of everything.

To truly find God, truth needs to be found independently from the opinions of others. The truth has to be found in our hearts; it has to be totally personal, totally in our inner aloneness. God is our inner core and is the core of everything. It is also the true guidance, which is always guiding us. If we are really interested in the truth we will find our own answers, because the truth reveals itself to the sincere heart as the guided unfolding of one's essence.

Usually, what I teach is an earnest personal inquiry into the truth of one's experiences, the truth of one's mind, the truth of one's consciousness, and the truth of reality. My experience is that reality is self-revealing. If we open ourselves to it, it will reveal its secrets to us. By sincerely inquiring about our experiences of ourselves and of the world, the resulting understanding itself will be the ever-expanding self-revelation of the mystery of existence.

The process of opening up to the God presence is a continuing one. I don't think of myself as having arrived at the final, ultimate truth. I feel that my experience is still limited and probably always will be, but will continue to grow and change. I do not see my experience of what God is or how to reach God as necessarily the final or the only way. I don't claim that kind of knowledge, nor do I know if anyone can. To me, that kind of knowledge is something that reveals itself over time. I do know that the moment essence is recognized as one's being, one's essential nature, and experienced as such, a radical transformation occurs. One's life and experiences of God will never be the same. No longer will God be experienced as something we were taught to believe in, but rather as something we can truly experience each moment of our lives.

An Invitation to God

by BARBARA DE ANGELIS, PH.D.

*"Ultimately, to me, an intimate relationship is
one of the most powerful pathways to God because it's
the path of the heart.... Following the path of the
heart requires surrender. Surrender doesn't mean
giving up, but yielding to something much greater."*

I HAVE ONLY ONE RELATIONSHIP — WITH GOD. God may be
disguised as my husband, my dog, the person driving
me crazy. Or God can come to me as the wind and the
weather. Truthfully, everything and everyone is a manifestation of God in different forms. My goal is to always be
in a relationship with God through everything I do.

When I was eighteen, I started on a conscious spiritual path. I studied with many teachers, and tried many
different practices, hoping to discover one that would
ultimately lead me to liberation. Finally, after more
than twenty-five years of earnest searching, I found a

consistent means of invoking and maintaining that inner awakening. I learned to meditate in a way that fosters my relationship with God, that allows me to know God within me *as* me. This practice has brought the richest, most grace-filled time of my life. Yet I know that every step along the way was necessary and precious, preparing me to recognize and receive this gift when it was revealed to me.

The biggest misunderstanding people have about God is thinking of God as a man in a white beard, who watches you, ready to punish your misdeeds and reward your good actions. This is far from the truth as I understand and have experienced it. When I started my search, I looked toward the Eastern traditions and gained a much broader understanding of a personal relationship with God. My search was for spirituality, not religion. Spirituality is about your own personal relationship with God. I found that God was not separate from me, was not some great concept beyond my reality or some being whom I needed an intermediary to contact. Indeed, *I was God*, an expression of God, a child of God. I began to understand that I didn't need to look for God outside myself and turned my search in the right direction: within. As my spiritual practices deepened, I had the most amazing revelation of God awareness inside myself. I felt a oneness with God. I didn't feel God outside, looking in, deciding whether or not to accept me. Instead, I felt God *in* me, expressing Itself through everything I did.

Another, very powerful way to experience God is through our relationships with others. The most important thing I try to teach people is that *the purpose of a relationship is not to make you feel good or even to make you happy. It's to help you grow and to bring you closer to God.*

I believe that an intimate relationship with another person is a profound opportunity for you to recognize all that is unloving in you, and to replace it with everything that's loving. Nothing can make you feel less enlightened than being in an intimate relationship. When you're single, it's easy to say, "I'm just so centered lately. I'm unconditionally loving toward everybody. I feel so good about myself. I have so much to give." Then you get into a relationship and four weeks later you're saying, *"This guy is driving me crazy! I feel like a wreck!"* Why? The universe has given you someone who shows you every part of yourself that's judgmental and critical, every part of you that isn't centered. So you have love, which makes you want physical, emotional, and spiritual union — and yet you have the array of personality traits that make you think, "We can't be one because I can't stand the way he chews."

Then in some moments two people *do* move from experiencing separateness to experiencing oneness. Many of these occur during lovemaking. This is the ultimate attraction of sex for people. In those moments all differences disappear and you're immersed in a sense of oneness. You experience such relief then because oneness is life's natural state, the larger truth. But when the sexual experience is over, the sense of joy and ecstasy leaves, and you think, "Well, to get it again, I have to have sex," or "I have to get someone to love me to feel that oneness." But what you've really experienced, and what you're really still looking for, is not sex, or even a relationship, but the experience of God-consciousness, of losing yourself in the ocean of God's love.

Ultimately, to me, an intimate relationship is one of the most powerful pathways to God because it's the path of the heart. God cannot be comprehended, understood, or experienced through the mind. In fact, the mind separates us from the God within because the mind identifies with who we *think* we are. I am a writer, say. I am a woman. I am a wife. I am smart. The path of the heart requires letting go of the mind, letting go of the ego, letting go of the "I," letting go of control.

Following the path of the heart requires surrender. Surrender doesn't mean giving up, but yielding to something much greater. It's an exquisite experience if we can find the courage to do it. Most people have a personal experience with God when something forces them to surrender. For instance, when standing on a mountaintop, the mind that normally says, "I am smart," or "I've accomplished so much" just can't maintain its sense of importance in the face of mountains so glorious, clouds so beautiful, and nature so exquisite in her perfection. In the face of all of that wonder, for a second, the mind just surrenders. And in that second, all of a sudden, you're filled with God. You think it's because of the mountains. It's really because you've surrendered. It's because you've allowed yourself to slip beneath your sense of who you are and taste the wonder.

Sometimes, too, this letting go happens through tragedy. You're in so much pain that you cry out, "I can't take it anymore." You've totally lost control. All of a sudden, you find yourself experiencing love or a tremendous grace, or feel a healing peace descending upon you.

You don't have to wait for these transcendental experiences to occur randomly. With practice, they can become a part of your everyday life. Many years ago I began practicing an inner exercise: I would have the intention to consciously notice when I wasn't connected inside, when I was feeling tense, separate, or contracted. I knew that at those moments I had disconnected from my center, that I had forgotten who I really was. I'd stop and intellectually remind myself to come back; I'd call on things I'd read, or even written myself; I'd call upon past moments of clarity; I'd call upon the truth, and in doing so, I'd make an effort to pull myself out of the swirling vortex of forgetfulness and return to center. After years of conscious practice, that process happens quite naturally. I don't have to force it.

I feel very, very fortunate because, after working on my own for so many years, I have finally found a spiritual teacher who has helped awaken my inner power and has kindled my inner flame, as the ancients say. This awakening created a radical shift in my being. Now, a consistent part of my awareness is conscious of my Self. I don't have to find my way back anymore. Instead, I simply have to notice that my attention has shifted in the wrong direction, away from God-consciousness within me and onto something that is creating suffering. Rather than feeling that I'm lost in a forest and have to find my way out, I remember that there is a beautiful and sacred clearing in which I can live, and if I ever wander off, I know exactly how to find my way back.

It was my teacher who showed me how to find the path to that clearing. A teacher is like the manual that comes with your computer. Perhaps you could master the computer without the manual, but it would take much longer. And in the case of a genuine spiritual teacher, she is more than just a collection of information or wisdom — she's the connecting wire that plugs her power source into yours.

It's important to choose your teacher carefully. The true guru respects the disciple or student. She honors her student as no different from herself, except that the guru has remembered who she is, while the student hasn't yet. The guru's job isn't to take you anywhere, but to help you remember your true identity. You are already God, love, and light. You just don't remember. A true teacher doesn't leave you feeling, "She is so fantastic, and I'm just such a piece of dirt." *To me, a true teacher is one in whose presence you remember and contact your own greatness.*

I want to tell you a story that, for me, illustrates what is essential about creating a relationship with God in your everyday life. This past summer, while attending a meditation retreat, I was sitting with several thousand people, waiting for my teacher to give a talk. I had just come out of a long period of meditation, and was in a fantastic state. I felt completely full and ecstatic.

The next speaker, who was a visiting professor, appeared and began his presentation. As I listened to him talk with great precision about some scholarly subject, I noticed a little thought creeping into my mind: "I don't think he's really being very effective. He's reading his talk — not giving it from the heart." I didn't pay much attention to this criticism, but a minute later I had another judgmental thought: "He's quoting a lot of esoteric references that people won't relate to."

And with that thought, I noticed my joyous state starting to contract. I began to feel restless and irritable; my body, which had been quite comfortable for hours, was hurting more. Then, all of a sudden, critical thoughts and judgments began pouring out of my mind — one after the other, like roaches creeping out of the woodwork. I watched in horror as my ego revealed itself in its full negative glory, until, at the end of ten minutes, I felt angry, dry, separate, empty, miserable, and completely devoid of love.

At that moment, my beloved teacher appeared, bringing with her an ocean of joy, laughter, and delight, which everyone proceeded to bathe in for the next hour — everyone but me. I couldn't feel her love because I had cut myself off from the love inside. I was stuck in the self-made hell of separation, and I remained there for the rest of the evening. I fled to my room at the end of the session and wept for hours, praying to be delivered from the prison of my own mind, praying that I would find my way back to love again.

This experience was one of the most painful, and yet most important, experiences of my life. In fact, it was a priceless gift. During that excruciating hour, I saw exactly how, with the tiniest critical thought, I separate myself from God. I separate myself from God's vision of love. I separate myself from my own loving heart. I'd never seen so clearly how much the mind's negativity can bury you in your own darkness. Seeing the contrast between my previous state of ecstasy and the subsequent state of agony, seeing this disintegration happen so quickly and dramatically, was indescribably profound and life-changing for me.

That experience showed me that I — from moment to moment — am the only person in control of my connection to God. It's not that God is deciding to connect with me or not connect with me, depending upon whether I had a good day, or did good or bad deeds. It's all up to me. God, the awareness of God, the love of God, the blessings of God — that lively ecstasy — is always there. It's me who separates from God by judging, by indulging in negativity, by criticizing myself, as well as others.

Since that experience, I have consciously practiced seeing God in every situation, in everyone. That's the first suggestion I'd like to offer you: Start to notice how many negative thoughts you have about things, situations, people (including yourself), and how you feel at the end of the day. If your day is full of little mean, dark thoughts, is it any wonder you feel crabby? Maybe it's not because things went wrong during your day. Maybe it's because you let your mind run wild like a dog putting its nose into garbage everywhere.

Once you become aware of your negative thoughts, practice replacing your dark thoughts with God-thoughts, right in the moment. Instantly, you'll experience a shift in your spiritual state. Instantly, you'll connect back to your own heart, back to the presence of God within.

Bringing God into your life is like wanting to have someone to your home. First you send the person an invitation. If it's a specific invitation, he or she is more apt to accept than if you say, "Oh, by the way, stop over any time." So, consciously, actively, send God an invitation. Go to the ocean or the mountains or a park, or light some candles at home. Wherever you decide to be, sit and say formally, *"God, I'm ready for you to reveal yourself in my life. I don't know how it's going to happen. I don't know if I'll recognize you when you get here, but I'm ready for a relationship with you. Send me signs. Send me the proper teacher. Send me the right path. Give me the wisdom to notice when these things arrive. Give me the strength and courage to travel down that path and begin to explore the invisible world."*

If you sincerely pray to experience God's presence into your life, it will come. The universe abhors a vacuum; if you create an opening, God will answer you. And remember, what you hear is the God within you, your own self. It's been waiting for the invitation.

Once you've offered that invitation, it's important to create opportunities for the invitation to be answered — moments when you are open to feeling God reveal Itself within you. To be in touch with God, you must make room for silence in your life. If you race around in the world, you won't have any quiet time. Without quiet time, during which you hear nothing but the sound of your own inner voice, you're not allowing yourself to feel God within you, speaking to you. It's like walking along a beautiful mountain trail with a big boom box blasting loud music. You won't hear the birds, the animals, the wind. So if you're constantly bombarded with sound and outer stimulation, you may not hear the messages coming from within you. The voice of the heart is very quiet.

Total quiet time is essential, even if it's five minutes driving in the car with your radio off. Try coming home and sitting in a quiet place, maybe lighting a candle and closing your eyes. If you don't have a meditation practice, just watch your thoughts, and notice the quiet places between the thoughts — they are the true self.

The inner voice, as I've experienced it, is very gentle and very subtle. You have to be still to hear it. It doesn't boom in your head. It doesn't necessarily speak in words. It's the language of the heart. It may come to you as a feeling to call someone. It doesn't have logic to it. It doesn't give you an outline with twenty-five reasons why.

A lot of us don't give ourselves a chance to hear what our heart is telling us because we're trying to hear through our mind. We think, "I sat there waiting for God to give me a message, but all that came was, 'I have to pick up my dry cleaning,' and, 'My back hurts,' and 'I should feed the cat.'" Maybe you think God is not communicating, but it only seems that way because you're waiting for God to speak through your mind, and that's not the abode of God. God will not appear through the mind, because the mind separates us from God.

Instead, give yourself time to listen to your heart. Have you ever had a feeling about something, ignored it, and ended up in big trouble? That feeling was a message from God. Each day, notice those feelings and honor them. Messages and calls and directions are always appearing if we pay attention. If you navigate by the map of the heart, miracles can happen in your life. If you let your mind talk you out of things that aren't logical, you're going to have a very boring life, because grace isn't logical. Love isn't logical. Miracles aren't logical.

Another important practice is to begin connecting with other people on a conscious spiritual path. The fellowship of like-minded people is a magnet that attracts grace. When you're around people who are committed to spiritual awakening, you begin resonating at the same level. Go to places that represent what you're looking for: a church, a meditation group — whatever feels right for you.

Finally, watch for God coming to you disguised in different forms. God expresses Itself through everything in creation. All of the universe serves as a mouthpiece for God. When the wind blows gently on you, it's God caressing you. When a friend gives you a kiss, it's God kissing you. When a dog greets you with enthusiasm, it's God greeting you. When the sun bathes you in its warmth, it's God shining down on you. The truth is, Grace is always already very present in your life.

.III.

꧁

Discovering
God

*"What matters is being spontaneously
open to the* reality *of God...."*

— Thomas Merton

Burning for God

by ANDREW HARVEY

"We must all understand that if we are to be divine,
we must, like the divine, love with divine intensity and
serve every sentient being on the earth."

EVERYTHING THAT HAPPENS, everything you feel, everything open to you through life is your relationship with God. Every sentient being has a spark of divine consciousness in them. Anyone born into this dimension is born with a hidden, direct connection with the total divine. The universe is our mother. Life is our mother. The events that happen in life are trying to mother us into deeper awareness. Our task is to wake up to this relationship, which is our birthright.

All the joys you experience, said Rumi, are rays from the sun of God. When you taste a delicious peach, you taste the body of God. The joy you feel looking at the face of your friend, your lover, or a child in the street is actually the soul's rapture at the presence of the divine in the universe. The music you thrill to is actually one facet of the great voice of the Creator. When you understand this, you understand that the divine is not far away from you, but is actually dancing fiercely in the core of your life at every moment.

To develop this understanding further, to create a deep personal relationship with God, we must take seriously the testimony of all the great mystics. They speak of this direct connection to the divine in ways that are astonishingly similar. Their testimony to the glory and passion and wildness and sometimes fierce suffering of this relationship is neither exaggeration nor poetry. They are simply explaining what all of us could live if we allowed the overwhelming love of God to come to us.

Fundamentally, there are three ways in which everyone can realize this direct relationship to the divine: prayer, meditation, and service. People say to me, "I find it so hard to pray." I respond, "Why don't you just talk to God? Talk to the image of God that moves you the most. Talk out of the depths of your present predicament. Know that you are heard and that a loving intelligence is trying to help you give birth to your deepest self." That's the evidence that all the mystics of all the traditions have given us. So, develop the habit of constant prayer. It is something anybody can do in any circumstance, and it's the core of the authentic spiritual life. There is nothing fancy about it at all. It's an extremely simple, extremely naked process.

It is essential that you combine prayer — talking to

God — with a very simple daily practice of meditation — listening to God. And, again, it's not complicated. You sit, with spine as straight as possible, and watch your thoughts. Try to imagine them as clouds passing across the sky. As the thoughts pass, the sky behind, with its vital, vibrant, pure light, remains. That light is your essential nature, and the essential nature of consciousness.

The advantage of practicing this simple meditation day in, day out, twenty minutes in the morning and twenty minutes before you go to bed is that you gradually establish a gap between your essential, divine nature, which is spacious, calm, joyful, blissful, full of tenderness toward all life, and the biographical self, which is caught in various karmic nightmares. Slowly, the gap between the essential you and the biographical you becomes easier to see. As this happens, you can exercise restraint and detachment, and gradually free your biographical self from the various obsessions that keep it fearful and blind. Then you can become more and more in harmony with your own richest spiritual possibilities.

But neither prayer nor meditation will help you much unless you constantly put what you learn about divine love into human practice. All the great sages, from Lao Tzu to Buddha to Confucius to Jesus, have told us that to experience the love of God we must give our love to those around us. We must give love to our families and friends first of all, but then to all the beings we meet in the course of a day and all the beings in the world. Everyone can find forms of service in the ordinary world to help them develop the quality of selfless love. That in turn brings them directly into the atmosphere of the divine. Prayer, meditation, and service, lived together, can engender the divine life if they are pursued with humility, reverence, and simplicity of heart.

Living them together, however, means resisting worldly pressures. We live in a culture that has created what I call the "concentration camp of reason," which denies the sacred. Because that culture has tremendous powers of bitter and banal persuasion, we've allowed ourselves to be intimidated out of our profound relationship with God. Modern life is incredibly stressful. Most people live lives of great financial and emotional insecurity. That, combined with the prevailing world view that denies the absolute and total reality of the miraculous and the mystical, makes it very hard for people to believe in and trust the divine.

Finding and making conscious the divine connection is very, very difficult. It is, however, something that everyone can do if they're prepared to work. Rama Krishna said, "People are always coming to me and saying, 'Why can't I see God? Why can't I feel God? Why can't I taste God?' And I always say to them, if you put into your spiritual life as much energy as you put into getting ahead in the office or in committing adultery or perfecting your lawn, then you'd have results. They may not come quickly, but they will come if you persist patiently."

That is the truth. There is no quick fix, no quick way to the relationship with God. But the time-honored ways of approaching God never fail if they are pursued with real sincerity. You discover that as you take one step toward the divine in openheartedness, the divine will take one thousand steps toward you. If you make one real, deep inner movement of the heart toward God, God will give you — or try to give you, as you must be willing to receive — all the signs necessary to show you that God is with you, that you are protected, that you are being instructed by your life and not defeated by it. People cannot experience this unless they're willing to take the leap, to take the chance.

I think one reason why people are so scared of taking that chance is that our culture spoon-feeds everything to us. If you want a television, you go out and work for it and you buy it. If you want to learn about Aztec pottery, you take a course. But the relationship with God requires the active and passionate participation of you, yourself. You have to risk it. You have to abandon yourself to it. You have to leap into the fire. Nobody will do it for you; nobody *can* do it for you. In a deep sense, we've all been made slaves of convenience by a culture that stresses ease and quick solutions. This has divorced us even more completely from our authentic self and from the rigors and risks of a real relationship with God.

Our task is to grow up and realize that to experience what the great mystics tell us is the truth of reality, we will have to risk something. If we open ourselves, become vulnerable, start in very humble ways to learn from the scriptures — to pray, to meditate, to serve — we will get definite results. This has been the experience of everyone who has taken this path. The journey is open to everyone, but everyone who takes it must give a great deal and, in certain circumstances, suffer a great deal.

There is a wonderful story, told, I believe, in Rama Krishna, that illustrates the need to give ourselves totally to God: A king is passing and sees a beggar with a bag of corn. The beggar says to the king, as he passes in his wonderful chariot, wearing his golden crown, "Oh, I'd love to give you something." The king says, "Well, why don't you give me all your corn?" The beggar responds, "Well, I can't give you all of it, but I'll give you five grains," to which the king says, "Fine." When the beggar returns home, he finds that five grains in his bag have turned to gold. He weeps as he realizes that had he given the whole bag of corn to the king, in an act of abandon, generosity, and trust, all of the grains would have turned to gold.

The same is true of all our external passions. If we truly give them to God, for God's own use, without our interference, not only will those external passions remain with us but they will be transfigured. A writer who writes for him- or herself can only experience the joys of the egocentric conquest of a language. But a writer who writes for the divine will make of that passion for writing an entrance into divine joy and illumination. A man who makes love to another simply for his own pleasure can only savor that passion from the one viewpoint of the ego. Those who understand, however, that lovemaking can reflect the divine energies of the universe, and who dedicate their lovemaking to an experience of this energy, will experience cosmic joy. And the experience will be far, far greater than anything physical pleasure could bring. So, the end result of giving one's passions to God is not having all the branches of life laid bare, but having them covered with ecstatic blossom.

Why, then, are we so frightened and mistrustful of surrendering to the divine? I think it's the fear of suffering. If you read the accounts of most authentic mystics, you see that the transition from ordinary human consciousness into divine human consciousness is always accompanied by trial, ordeal, and renunciation; sometimes by disease and extreme physical suffering; and nearly always by great mental distress. Any transformation in nature costs a lot; every resurrection is proceeded by a crucifixion. I think when people begin to intuit what will be demanded of them — not by a sadistic, cruel God, but by the law of growth in the universe — they become terrified. They see that living for God will involve a kind of death. That is why the practices of prayer, meditation, and service are so important — those practices can open a being to the miracle of divine love and help that being love enough to, in turn, suffer enough to be transformed.

For me, what matters most is that as I've grown in this experience, I feel more and more humbled before the majesty of God. I feel simultaneously more divine and more human. I feel more completely awake to my divine potential, yet also more aware of my human failings. My own inner experience is that the deeper the awakening, the greater the sense of human incompetence. That in turn brings a greater need to surrender to divine grace and to divine help.

In my own journey, I went through three main stages. At the beginning, I didn't believe in anything. That was a stage of anger, bitterness, despair, and denial. In the second stage, I had profound mystical experiences, which opened my being but also gave me an overly grandiose and glamorous impression of myself *to* myself.

I was lucky: a great shattering occurred that started to divorce me from everything I had pursued, all my visions of myself. This purification resulted in a much more realistic relationship with God; it is a much closer union, in which awe and humility and profound gratitude play a constant part. And it's that relationship that I hope to deepen until my last breath.

In the third stage, the real experience of God goes far beyond any kind of bliss or awakening; in a certain way it actually is a very ordinary experience. It is simply a commitment to bring love into every detail of one's life and being and thought and emotion. This is much less glamorous but much more truthful to the real life of God. To reach this point, the false spiritual self must be crushed. It's a painful and horrifying experience, but one that must be experienced to realize two things: how you are nothing and, simultaneously, one with the power that rules the universe. These two recognitions must go hand in hand, to prevent you from either despairing completely by realizing that you are nothing, or giving yourself ludicrous airs of divinity, which is what many modern seekers and masters do. We are not divine; we are at once human and divine. Whatever stage of emotion we reach, there is always more work to be done, more love to give and experience.

Emphasis on giving and receiving love is crucial. So

many people go through the spiritual life to attain detachment, to avoid the pain of reality. This is a disaster, because nature is burning, two billion people are living in poverty, half the earth's species have been destroyed, television is an avalanche of trash and vulgarity, and our quality of life is degrading beyond belief. In the meantime, the New Age is talking about how everything is being transformed and a new world is beginning. Nothing is beginning, and nothing *can* begin until the rigor and splendor of the authentic mystical life is taken extremely seriously. We must all understand that if we are to be divine, we must, like the divine, love with divine intensity and serve every sentient being on the earth.

Many people are driven toward religion seeking solace. This isn't a true relationship with God. You're essentially asking God to serve as a drug pusher to provide you with the bliss and consolation you need to get through. God is love, but a love that creates and serves. If you come into authentic connection with that love, your whole being undergoes a painful revolution. Very few people want to go through that. They want all the glory without the grit, all the gold without the sweat and the blood. It's simply not possible. The divine will not sell itself cheaply. The way to realize divine love and action is through the cross. The way is through annihilation. The way is through abandoning the games and petty satisfactions of the ego.

A wonderful story by Henry James describes what happens when someone tries to avoid the true trials of the journey to the divine. Early in the story, a man is told that something terrible is going to happen to him. So, he withdraws, hardly sees anybody, and lives a very, very protected existence. One day, while walking in a cemetery, he sees an old woman throwing herself on the grave of her husband, weeping and calling out. Suddenly, witnessing her grief and the love that lay under it, he realizes that the terrible thing he would experience was that *nothing* would ever happen to him. The woman showed him a love that is the glory of life. That glory would never be his because of his fear. It's a wonderful story, and everyone's story. To be open is to risk being shattered, but without that shattering there is no glory. As Rumi wrote:

> *The Burning Bush has come. It must put us to the test.*
> *We wanted revelation and now we must burn.*
> *You said "yes" at the beginning, why do you shrink now?*
> *Become a salamander. Make a house of fire.*

(This essay was adapted from an interview with Benjamin Shield, Ph.D.)

Leaning Toward the Light

by STEPHEN LEVINE

꧁

*"It may be said that God cannot be known
in the mind but only experienced in the heart."*

WHEN I WAS THIRTEEN I attended a summer camp run by a gentle bear of a man who was a Christian Scientist. My time with him was among my first introductions to the experience of the divine. His being displayed an ethic and a mercy I had not previously noticed in the world around me. One day I received a phone call from my parents, who were very angry because a neighbor told them he thought I had stolen something from him. My parents were outraged and insisted I make amends immediately.

Because I received the call in the camp office, the camp director overheard some of the conversation. He noticed the fear and the distress I was experiencing. After I hung up the phone he put his arms around me. I put my head on his chest and sobbed. As I cried, he held me and said, "Everything will be all right. Just take a breath or two. Everything will be all right." And as he comforted me I looked toward the wall and saw a framed embroidery that read, "God is Love." I remember very clearly, at that moment, understanding something about God's nature I had never before comprehended. I realized that what this man offered me was God itself, was mercy, was nonjudgment and unconditional acceptance of me, simply as a human being in all the throes and flows a human experiences on the way to completion.

Many years later, in my course of an expanding commitment to self-discovery and service, Ramana Maharishi reminded me repeatedly that "God, Guru, and Self are one." As my practice deepened, feelings of separation from God diminished. And when that nauseating anxiety would momentarily manifest, it increasingly melted into God itself — a gradually deepening experience of the vastness of being shared with all there is and all that ever will be. In going beyond separation, beyond the self that strives even to know, there was a peace and a happiness I had seldom known.

Some years ago, while I was involved in an arduous Buddhist meditation practice, the door opened to the room in my mind in which I was sitting and in walked the luminescent figure of Jesus. I was dismayed. "You must have the wrong guy. I'm a Buddhist. Maybe you're looking for the fellow down the hall!" He smiled with the smile of the heart that knows no separation. His presence suffused the room with the infinite mercy of the shared heart. He motioned to be still and to listen. My mind, full of rigid knowing, burst to expose the sacred heart beating in my chest. I was ecstatic for days.

In the direct experience of the shared heart I experienced The Deathless, that which precedes birth and extends beyond death. Asked afterward what that experience was all about, in exasperation I could say only that it was the experience of God, of our God nature, of our underlying reality, the ocean of being on which floats the tiny waves of thought and personality.

Since that time I have found myself often using the term "God." I am very comfortable with that term because I don't have the foggiest idea what it means. But I see no place where it is absent. Indeed, it may be said that God cannot be known in the mind but only experienced in the heart. You cannot know God; you can only be God. Thus you cannot know "the truth" but only enter directly the moment in which truth resides. Truth is an experience, a sip at the deep well of being, not a cluster of words or thoughts or even insights in the mind.

There is in all our strivings a profound homesickness for God. When we touch another we touch God. When we look at a flower, its radiance, its fragrance, its stillness is another moment's experience of something deeper within. When we hold a baby, when we hear extraordinary music, when we look into the eyes of a great saint, what draws us is that deep homesickness for our true nature, for the peace and healing that is our birthright. This homesickness for God directs us toward the healing we took birth for, the coming into pure being that out of a poverty of language we describe as God. But God is not "God" any more than a flower is not "Flower." God is the direct experience of our true nature just as a flower is the direct experience of the miracle of germination and color and the indescribable beauty of simply being.

However, in a sense there is no such thing as "going home to God." We are already in the living room. All we need do is sit comfortably in the chair that awaits. Or, as my wife, Ondrea, put it, "The arms of the mother are always around you. All you need do is put your head on her shoulder."

Sometimes when I read a poem by Rumi or Kabir tears rise for the absolute joy of our journey toward ourselves. Because our true nature had no edge on it, no limit or limitation, it is impossible to describe its direct experience, because all description is based on duality: if it's short it's not tall, if it's white it's not black, if it's high it's not low. But in that experience of limitless being there is no reference point, no duality, no one separate from God to describe the experience. It is an emerging, a dissolving, a dying into our true nature.

It is for the love of God that we love. It is for the mercy of God that we go beyond judgment. It is into the sacred heart of our own divinity that we sojourn as through Dante's classic inferno to recapture and reexperience the ground of being on which we walk our tremulous way through a confusing life of the mind. God is not to be found in the mind, and the mind is all that separates us from God. Indeed, if you make a list of all that you hold precious, of all that you fear losing, of all that you think you are, of all that gains you praise and guards you from blame, you would have a list of your separations from God. You would have a list of all that the mind protects, defends, attempts to maintain in a false solidity, in all it keeps to maintain its separate reality.

Our experiences have all been within the stream of flow and change; every thought, every moment of tasting, of touching, of thinking, of hearing, of smelling has had a beginning, a middle, and an end. Only one experience in all our lives has been constant: the experience of simply being. Since the moment we become aware that we are aware, whether in the womb, at birth, or at the breast, there has underlain all the phenomena of thought and feeling simply the hum of being. My experience of being and your experience of being are exactly the same — the boundaryless, wordless whoosh of suchness. But when I am being this and you are being that, heaven and hell are set infinitely apart, holy wars arise, and starvation ensues. When you and I are no longer "you and I" but just the oneness that permeates all, that one constant of simply being that all experience, that underlying ocean of being on which our tiny selves float is easily described as God.

And I see, after more than twenty years of Buddhist meditation practice, that we watch our minds to see who we aren't. For God is found beyond the mind, when conditioned responses part and one goes beyond the seeming to the real. It is our willingness to be healed, to be at one with something deeper than personality or separate aggrandizement that does the work that is to be done. To die out of separation into the unity, the oneness, the suchness of being takes us past the mind to the heart of the matter. In that experience there is a sense of "reality" hardly paralleled by any previous experience.

One of our teachers said that the practice of discovering the divine was the practice of remembering — to remember to be mindful of the contents of the mind so as to see beyond; to remember to be present in those moments when the mind is so full that the heart is least available; to remember, as Thomas Merton said, that "true love and prayer are learned in the moments when prayer has become impossible and the heart has turned to stone."

There are many ways to aid remembering. I find that nothing helps me "remember God" as much as daily meditation practice. For some time each day, or a few times a day, Ondrea and I sit, watching the breath and noticing the movement of mind as it comes and goes but does not distract from the sacred spaciousness that is our birthright.

One morning I awoke on my side and thought, I must get up now and meditate. But very quickly I wondered what would happen if someday I couldn't get up and meditate. What happens if I come to a point in my life where lying on my side, half-embryonic, is the only position available to me. Would I then no longer be able to experience God? So I began to meditate upon awakening without changing posture, sometimes for twenty minutes, sometimes for three hours before I had to get up. I lay there watching my mind's idiosyncratic desire to alleviate the discomfort that may have arisen from maintaining one posture and its desire to let go of the fears, the old holdings, the absence of delight at being in a situation over which it may have no control.

In Zen there is a wonderful statement: "Spring comes and the grass grows all by itself." That statement shows us the wisdom of letting go of all the attempts to maintain control and hide from our pain (which thus turns it to suffering). To let go of control is to enter into creation in the act of becoming. We discover who we have always been when we stop attempting to become better than who we really are. The very desire to be better than who we are is to have forgotten God. We need not be one iota different to directly experience the absolute vastness of our true being. In going beyond the mind, beyond that which blocks the heart, we discover who we have always been and always will be.

Now I do not notice the ecstatic commune I once experienced so regularly. Rather, I experience a constant hum of quietness and confidence in my true nature. What was once at the center of my life — my love of God and of deepening self-awareness — has now permeated to the edges, has become more integrated, more "common." In many ways the most consistent experience now is that sense of spacious ease that is my true nature, and so much less the rapid roller-coaster ups and downs of feeling at one with God and then feeling so distant from God. Now there is just a sense that when I am present God is present. When I am wholeheartedly in the moment nothing is separate from God.

Even in the hellish states of mind that we all experience at times and may feel locked into for extended periods, there is indeed God. Beneath the vicissitudes of thought and feeling and image and remembrance is a spaciousness, a mercy, a delight in being that goes beyond comprehension.

It seems that God becomes more solid the more we need that experience; but when the experience is integrated into just being, when being is enough and nothing is absent or called for, then God is less form. Indeed, it is hard not to be an impostor when one speaks of God, for one almost needs to create something separate from God in order to view God. But when there is nothing separate, no clinging or condemning, when there is no desire for control or evasion, then all that remains is God.

Encounter with God Through the Senses

by Brother David Steindl-Rast

"In my best, most alive moments — in my mystical moments — I have a profound sense of belonging."

WHEN SOMEONE ASKS ME about my personal relationship with God, my spontaneous reply is a question: What do you mean by God? For decades I have spoken about religion with people all over the world, and I have learned that the word "God" must be used with utmost caution if we want to avoid misunderstandings. I also find far-reaching agreement among human beings when we reach that mystical core from which all religious traditions spring. Even those who cannot identify with organized religion are often deeply rooted in mystical experience. This is where I find my reference point for the meaning of the term "God." The term must be anchored in that mystical awareness in which all humans agree before they start talking about it.

In my best, most alive moments — in my mystical moments — I have a profound sense of belonging. At those moments I am aware of being truly at home in this universe. There is no longer any doubt in my mind that I belong to this Earth Household, in which each member belongs to all others — bugs to beavers, black-eyed Susans to black holes, quarks to quails, lightning to fire-flies, humans to hyenas. To say yes to this limitless mutual belonging is love. When I speak of God, I mean this kind of love, this great yes to belonging. I experience this love at one and the same time as God's Yes to all that exists. In saying yes, I realize God's very life and love within me.

But there is more to this yes of love than a sense of belonging. There is always also a deep longing. Who has not experienced in love both the longing and the belong-ing? Paradoxically, these two heighten each other's inten-sity. The more intimately we belong, the more we long to belong ever more fully. Longing adds a dynamic aspect to our yes of love. The fervor of our longing becomes the expression and the very measure of our belonging. Noth-ing is static; everything is in motion with a dynamism that is, moreover, deeply personal.

When love is genuine, belonging is always mutual. The beloved belongs to the lover, as the lover belongs to the beloved. I belong to this universe and to the divine Yes that is its Source, and this belonging is also mutual. That is why I can say "my God" — not in a possessive sense, but in the sense of a loving relatedness. Now, if my deepest belonging is mutual, could my most fervent long-ing be mutual, too? It must be so. Staggering though it is, what I experience as my longing for God is God's longing for me. One cannot have a personal relationship with an impersonal force. True, I must not project on God the limitations of a person; yet, the Divine Source must have all the perfections of personhood. Where else would I have gotten them?

It makes sense, then, to speak of a personal relationship with God. We are aware of this — dimly at least — in moments in which we are most wakeful, most alive, most truly human. And we can cultivate this relationship by cultivating wakefulness, by living our lives to the fullest.

The Bible expresses these insights in the words "God speaks." "God speaks" is one way of pointing toward my personal relationship with the Divine Source. This relationship can be understood as a dialogue. God speaks, and I am able to answer.

But how does God speak? Through everything there is. Every thing, every person, every situation, is ultimately Word. The Word tells me something and challenges me to respond. Each moment with all that it contains spells out the great yes in a new and unique way. By making my response, moment by moment, word by word, I am becoming the Word that God speaks in me and to me and through me.

That is why wakefulness is so preeminent a task. How can I give a full response to this present moment unless I am alert to its message? And how can I be alert unless all my senses are wide awake? God's inexhaustible poetry comes to me in five languages: sight, sound, smell, touch, and taste. All the rest is interpretation — literary criticism, as it were, not the poetry itself, because poetry resists translation. It can be fully experienced only in its original language, all the more true of divine poetry of sensuousness. How, then, can I make sense of life if not through my senses?

When and to what do our senses respond most readily? If I ask myself this question, I think immediately of working in my small garden. For fragrance, I grow jasmine, pineapple mint, sage, thyme, and eight kinds of lavender. What an abundance of delightful smells on so small a patch of ground! And what a variety of sounds: spring rain, autumn wind, year-round birds — mourning dove, blue jay, and wren; the hawk's sharp cry at noon and the owl's hooting at nightfall — the sound the broom makes on gravel, wind chimes, and the creaking garden gate. Who could translate the taste of a strawberry or fig into words? What an infinite array of things to touch, from the wet grass under my bare feet in the morning to the sun-warmed boulders against which I lean when the evening turns cool. My eyes go back and forth between the near and the far: the golden green metallic beetle lost among rose petals, the immense expanse of the Pacific, rising from below the cliff to the far-off horizon where sea and sky meet in mist.

Yes, I admit it. To have a place of solitude like this is an inestimable gift. It lets the heart expand, lets the senses wake up, one by one, to come alive with fresh vitality. Whatever our circumstances, we need somehow to set aside a time and a place for this kind of experience. It is a necessity in everyone's life, not a luxury. What comes alive in those moments is more than eyes or ears; our hearts listen and respond. Until I attune my senses, my heart remains dull, sleepy, half dead. In the measure in which my heart wakes up, I hear the challenge to rise to my responsibility.

We tend to overlook the close connection between responsiveness and responsibility, between sensuousness and social challenge. Outside and inside are of one piece. As we learn to really look with our eyes, we begin to look with our hearts also. We begin to face what we may prefer to overlook, begin to see what is going on in this world of ours. As we learn to listen with our ears, our hearts begin to hear the cry of the oppressed. To be in touch with one's body is to be in touch with the world — that includes the Third World and all other areas with which our dull hearts are conveniently out of touch.

In my travels I notice how easy it is to lose attentiveness. Oversaturation of our senses tends to dim our alertness. A deluge of sense impressions tends to distract the heart from single-minded attention. But the hermit in each of us does not run away from the world; it seeks that Stillpoint within, where the heartbeat of the world can be heard. All of us — each in a different measure — need solitude, because we need to cultivate mindfulness.

How shall we do this in practice? Is there a method for cultivating mindfulness? There are many methods. The one I have chosen is gratefulness, which can be practiced, cultivated, learned. And as we grow in gratefulness, we grow in mindfulness. Before I open my eyes in the morning, I remind myself that I have eyes to see while millions of my brothers and sisters are blind — most because of conditions that could be improved if our human family would come to its senses and spend its resources reasonably, equitably. If I open my eyes with this thought, chances are that I will be more grateful for the gift of sight and more alert to the needs of those who lack that gift. Before I turn off the light in the evening, I jot down one thing for which I have never before been grateful. I have done this for years, and the supply still seems inexhaustible.

Gratefulness brings joy to my life. How could I find joy in what I take for granted? So I stop "taking for granted," and there is no end to the surprises I find. A grateful attitude is a creative one, because, in the final analysis, opportunity is the gift within the gift of every moment — the opportunity to see and hear and smell and touch and taste with pleasure.

There is no closer bond than the one that gratefulness celebrates, the bond between giver and thanksgiver. Everything is a gift. Grateful living is a celebration of the universal give-and-take of life, a limitless yes to belonging.

Can our world survive without gratefulness? Whatever the answer, one thing is certain: to say an unconditional yes to the mutual belonging of all beings will make this a more joyful world. This is the reason why Yes is my favorite synonym for God.

Open to the Great Mystery

by BROOKE MEDICINE EAGLE

"Spirit lives in you; it lives within your body, in every cell. You can touch the Great Spirit by touching into your own aliveness."

MY RELATIONSHIP WITH GOD developed at an early age. I was raised on a remote little ranch, where I had for company and for the fullness of my life three other humans and an enormous amount of animals and land and sky and wind. As a child, my experience of God included everything — a love of the whole beauty around me. And the country was so beautiful: mountains that ended in aspen groves and streams, thick with wild animals and game of all kinds. One time I said to my mother, "You know, I think heaven is just like this, only the animals would speak to us; they wouldn't be afraid of us."

In developing a personal relationship with the Great Spirit, you first pay attention to the fact that you already

97

have a relationship with Spirit. Spirit is not something far off that you need to seek or call or grab or go to Tibet to find. Spirit lives in you; it lives within your body, in every cell. You can touch the Great Spirit by touching into your own aliveness. All you need is a different attitude about how big you are, how deep you are, how high you are. You must be willing to own that you are God; even though you are a minute part of the All That Is, you are connected and one with it.

It is also good for you to develop another kind of attention and ability: to hold more and more of life, more and more of the holiness, the whole circle. An elder once asked me, "How long has it been since we sang in celebration of the life of the great whale? How long has it been since we danced in celebration of the life of the flowers? How long has it been since we danced in celebration of each and every part of life?" It's been much too long.

When we are newborns, we have attention only for our mothers. Our little faces look into their faces and that's all we see. Then perhaps father gets connected in; then the other siblings. Our ability to love or pay attention to or be connected with things begins to expand. We may belong to a clan or a group, and we can expand our arms and hold all its members inside our circle. Sometimes we become big enough to hold more, perhaps big enough to be called a Mother of the City. This person loves all the people, the whole city; loves and holds them in a good way and does good things in honor of them. Some people are Mothers of Nations. As we expand our attention, we have the kind of love that can hold something that big. Mother Earth is enormous compared to that kind of love. She is big enough and loving enough to hold all of us in her arms all the time. When we expand our attention to the Great Mystery, to the All That Is — which is in and attentive to everything, because every cell, every tiny bit of matter, has consciousness in it — then we have an omniscient, omnipresent, powerful experience. We must build the ability to do that. When we talk about moving toward God realization, that's where we're moving.

When I speak about attention, I mean literally, "How much attention can we pay to ourselves?" As children, sometimes we cannot hold our attention for more than a couple of seconds. Over the years we are able to attend to more and more. Yet, we're seldom schooled to hold life in respect, to enlarge our ability to love, take care of, and be respectfully connected with all things around us. In the old days, the primary job of the native Lakota mother was to teach the new child that he or she was connected with everything in the circle of life. She would take the child walking and say, "See the squirrel? That's your brother. See the tree? We are related. This is your family; these are all your family." Because they were all brought up that way, they knew deeply that they were all interconnected, they were all family, they were all conscious. Lakota children had an opportunity to begin early in life to attend to the whole or the holiness, the spiritual side of things, and then to expand this ability powerfully as they grew.

We, too, can acknowledge that Spirit lives within us, that we are a part of God. The more we can love ourselves and attend to all of life around us with a loving, open, connected heart and good relationship, the more we can be in a very beautiful place. All it takes is practice.

Dialogue also is important in relating to the Great Spirit. It's not just my talking to the enormous All That Is. The All That Is also talks to me — gives me information, support, nurturance, food. It's a totally open connection. In the Sacred Pipe of our Lakota people, the bowl represents the earth and all of life. The open wooden stem represents our eternal connection to the Great Spirit. The pipe has an open channel that our breath or vibration or energy or thought can go through. Not only can it go out, but it can also come in. When we breathe through the pipe, it's like drawing Spirit into us. We can draw in information, and we can send out whatever we want across the bridge to everything else by blowing out the smoke or by praying with just our breath, energy, thoughts, and gratitude.

The channel is open in everyone. No one, whether priest or medicine man, needs to intercede or interpret or make that bridge any better, more open, more clear, more truthful, more sacred, or more holy. We have an open channel to the deepest, most beautiful part of ourselves, which is the same as our connection with everything. You don't need someone to put a hand on your head and say, "Yes, you're okay, and now you can talk to God." This priestly attitude assumes that you are not already in touch with Spirit and capable in that realm, although perhaps you may not be so practiced as some. That bridge to Spirit is always there, always open. You never need to stand at a tollgate on that bridge.

It's wonderful to be in the energy of elders and others who are practiced in that relationship with God. When that connection is humming, it's like a song going on. The elders give you suggestions and pray with you and hold you in their energy and light and wisdom as you go upon the mountain and have your own unique and powerful connection with Spirit.

It is very hard on people to assume that they don't have the ability to make that spiritual contact directly. It is sad that in the wider culture — and even now in native cultures, because of the breakup of old ways — there are very few who have the breadth and depth of attention to be holy people. Think how powerful it would be if our mothers really acknowledged, and were grateful for, our connection to everything. We would have turned out very differently.

Hologram theory offers a powerful example about who we are and who God is. A holographic picture is three dimensional. If you tear the picture in half, each half retains the same image and is still three dimensional. If you tear one of those halves in half, you still have the same dimensional image. No matter how many times you tear the fragments in half, the same image is still there. The tinier you tear it and the more times you tear it, the dimmer it gets, the less distinct and real it becomes to your eyes.

I am and you are and we all are individual tiny pieces

— all individuated or torn up out of the sheet that is God, that is All That Is. The whole picture is connected in us. It's all here. My little scrap may be torn to look a little different, but the whole picture is, in fact, within me. The exciting thing is that I can make that picture more distinct by joining my piece with your piece, and then with my family's piece, and then with my friend's piece, and on and on. The more I can attend to or connect myself with everything else around me, the more distinct the pictures become for us all. And we can reach out to others in the same way. Together we can acknowledge and enlarge our attentions so that we stand in a holy place — in a place that takes in the whole circle, a place that is healed in this wholeness, this holiness, a world that is healed and complete.

God as Global Love

by BARBARA MARX HUBBARD

"I believe that the transformation of the world is happening. . . ."

WHEN I FIRST EXPERIENCED AN AWARENESS of God, at about age eighteen, I didn't call it "God." I was raised as a materialistic agnostic. I only knew, at the time, that I felt a magnetic attraction toward something that was pulling me out of my life pattern. Because I didn't know what was attracting me, and because my secular background didn't support it, I felt this pull as an anguish. For many years I tracked that pull, calling it "a pull for greater meaning, greater purpose in my life," but I couldn't embrace it until many years later.

One day in 1966 I had the first of what I call a "peak-spiritual experience," which set me on the path of my relationship with God. I was taking a walk on a hill and thinking about what I'd been reading by Reinhold Niebuhr on the subject of community. He had quoted St.

Paul: "All men are members of one body." Holding this idea in my consciousness, I silently asked the universe a question: "What is our story? What in our age is comparable to the birth of Christ?"

With that question in mind, I went on a kind of day-dream-like walk. Suddenly I had an experience that was similar to a movie playing in my mind. It was as if I were witnessing myself and everyone else as cells within the living body of Gaia, and in that instant I felt that I had become a cell in the living body of the whole. In my mind's vision the waters of the earth cleared up, the weapons dissolved, and the food coursed through the planetary body. I heard the words, "Our story is a birth. It is a birth of humanity as one body."

The first step in my relationship with God was an inner experience of being part of a living whole. This experience led me to understand that we are participants in the process of Creation. We are both created by it and co-creative with it. The ultimate destiny of the human race is to take another quantum jump, just as from non-life to life or from animal life to human life. I began to see that however small we are, we each have our own relationship with God. I experienced that voice, or vision, as it were, as a voice of God that was beyond myself, yet simultaneously related to me.

I started to meditate and ask questions of the voice. I cultivated an inner voice of God, which I've since learned is in all of us and can be heard at all times, if only we learn to listen. I became aware that I am constantly in touch with that Source of the Creation. That voice of God began training me to get over my feelings of separation and activated me to begin a profound mission: to tell the story of humanity as one body being born to our new relationship with God as partners and co-creators. I went back to the Biblical realization, "We are created in the image of God." I realized that if I saw myself as separate and unworthy, then I was actually being sacrilegious, because I was a creation of God. By acknowledging myself as an aspect of God, I was being humble rather than egotistical. I kept getting deep signals about how I was part of the process of Creation. I could experience warmth. I could experience joy. I could experience being supported by the Force of God itself.

As I read the Scriptures and allowed myself to write, an interesting idea was put forward to me: Armageddon is what would happen if self-centered consciousness continued because we cannot inherit the power that is ours to inherit if we remain self-centered humans. However, because many millions have experienced such a rise of consciousness now, Armageddon is no longer necessary. The alternative is a "planetary Pentecost" — a time when we all hear from within, in our own languages, the mighty works of God and humanity. The division of the religions would be over. The separation of humanity from God would be over. We would each know that God is within us. I saw that my cosmic birth experience was a precognition of a planetary event that is to come if we, as human beings, choose to simultaneously join in the upper realm of consciousness.

The solution to our physical problems of the

environment, hunger, poverty, and injustice will be resolved through experiencing ourselves as one. It cannot be resolved by linear, materialistic means alone. In our joining, the new technologies of science will be transformed from weaponry and competition to creativity, restoration, and love of all life on a universal scale.

Although I have received many inner instructions about how to be in touch with God, the essential message is always the same: to be aware that Christ is our potential self and to mirror ourselves in His image. How does He see life, how does He feel, how does He love, how does He create something out of nothing? By bringing this light Presence into my life I gradually transmuted my sense of separation, so that now I feel I am on the path of being a co-creator.

The way to becoming a co-creator is, first, to meditate in silence at least once a day. Have a journal present. In the deepest silence and relaxation of your being, ask for anything to come forward — any information from God on any question you have. After a while you will feel an inner knowing bubbling up from within you. Sometimes it will be images, sometimes feelings, sometimes words. But however you get it, write it down.

You will discover that the inner voice can educate your rational, linear, critical mind to quiet down enough so that you become aware that the wisdom of God is within you.

The next step is to learn to speak with one another as our own inner voices of God. A small group of people — the "core group" — is the key practice for me now. We join together based on the inner desire to create something positive in the world. In the safety and security of a small group, when the inner listening and inner speaking takes place, our Higher Selves can come forth out of hiding.

The final step is to learn to work together from the core of our connectiveness as expressions of God. I believe that the transformation of the world is happening to those individuals willing to transform themselves together as expressions of God in their work.

A twenty-first century interpretation of the New Testament is that we are in the process of an evolutionary jump from creature-separated Homo sapiens to cocreative universal humanity. This jump was expressed in the Old and New testaments and was described as "the New Jerusalem," as the time beyond sorrow, beyond separation, and beyond death that we are heading toward. In the last two thousand years, this revelation has been unfolding. Our generation has inherited the power that was predicted in the New Testament: the power to destroy this world or — if aligned with the will of God — to evolve this world. Our time of transformation will be in partnership only with a cosmic Being who is literally present in all of us at all times. We won't transform by secular, materialistic means alone.

The great yogis, the Hindu religion, the Buddhists, and the Muslims all predicted and prepared us for this transformation. I envision not just an ecumenical joining of the religions, but rather a fulfillment of the vision of all the religions, with the Old and New testaments being evolutionary components of our spiritual relationship with God.

If all who feel we are connected to each other, to nature, and to God join in a planetary Pentecost, we shall be transformed together in this lifetime. I believe in the peaceful Second Coming as the solution to the world — not the exclusive Coming in which people will be destroyed, but the inclusive Coming, in which God in the heart of everyone will gently rise and we shall all be changed.

Awakening to the Dharma

by JOSEPH GOLDSTEIN

*"Cultivating an active mindfulness of one's
experience, moment to moment, is the path to awakening."*

I HAD MY FIRST CONTACT WITH BUDDHISM and meditation when I went to Thailand. The first time I sat in meditation was for just five minutes, but even that glimpse was exciting and transformative. It opened a new possibility of understanding. I saw that almost everything else I had studied had been an exploration of externals. This experience of meditation turned my attention around: It gave me a sense that there is actually a path through inner experience, and this has been borne out in ways I hadn't dreamed of at that time.

For me the word "God" refers to something quite different from what may be meant in different traditions. Buddhism does not have a theistic notion of God as a being outside oneself. In the Buddhist tradition, the word that most closely translates as God is "Dhamma" ("Dharma" in Sanskrit), which means "Truth" or "Reality." This includes the truth or reality of our everyday experiences as well as the transcendent truth of the unconditioned, which is beyond the phenomena we normally know, beyond all our normal ways of thinking.

Most of us live in a world of conceptual perception. We put names and language on our experiences, often confusing those concepts with the experience itself. The practice of the Dhamma has as its goal a clear awareness in each moment of experience as it actually is, a state where one can drop beneath the level of concept to a clearer seeing of things as they truly are. For example, I may be sitting in meditation and start to feel some pain. In a usual mode of perception, I may think, "My back hurts" or "My knee hurts." In doing so, I create a concept of a knee or a back as well as a concept of the self who is experiencing that pain. In an intimate connection with the Dhamma, however, I drop these concepts and become one with the simple sensation that is arising in the body.

As I drop into this nonconceptual level, I perceive the process of these elements of experience differently, particularly in periods of intense meditation. For example, I may be looking at my desk. On the level of *concept* I may see desk; on the level of *direct perception* I may see color and form. On the level of deep concentrated *awareness*, however, I may see a reality that is not normally available to ordinary perception, just as when we view things through an electron microscope a new level of reality becomes apparent. On this unusually deep level, one sees constantly changing elements with no solid core, continuously arising and dissolving — being born and dying. There is absolutely nothing static, secure, or substantial within them. As we observe the mind and body in this way, we come to a different kind of understanding. The notion of I or self or solidity of the body completely disappears.

When this awareness is practiced continuously, we come into an increasingly deeper connection with the Truth, or the Dhamma. This connection also brings about a deep balance of mind from which we may experience that which goes beyond what we can know through the senses and through the mind. This is what Buddhism calls the "Unconditioned" or "Nibbana" (in Sanskrit, "Nirvana"). This transcendent experience is difficult to talk about conceptually, because words cannot express what is not known via our normal senses. When the mind reaches a certain place of balance, it can open to what is beyond the process of incessantly changing mental and physical elements altogether, coming to a place of stillness, silence, and peace. The Buddha called this "the unborn, the undying." He said that here earth, air, water, and fire do not arise; length, breadth, change, and imperfection could not be. We know the true nature of the Dhamma in this opening, and we know it when we are following the path leading to this realization.

Deep experiences of the Dhamma have changed the reference point for most of my day-to-day experiences. I had perceived experience as referring to a self, to someone who was having it, for example, "I'm thinking" or "I feel angry, happy." Everything referred to a sense of "I." Now, instead of referring to a self, experiences seem to be more a sense of simply "phenomena arising and passing" without anyone behind them to whom they are happening.

A short teaching of the Buddha expresses this idea succinctly: "In the seen, there is just what is seen, in the heard, there is just what is heard, in the sensed (smell, taste, and touch), there is just what is sensed, and in thought there is just what is thought."

An amazing simplicity comes when we no longer create the concept of self or I behind experience. Life becomes so much less identified with any particular thought, sensation, emotion, or situation as being I. We are no longer imprisoned by the tight and narrow construct of self. With this awareness, our experiences become spacious and peaceful.

The process of understanding "selflessness" is progressive. There are still times when other forces, such as greed or anger or fear, may arise in the mind; there may still be temporary identifications with these elements. Although the root of self-idea has been cut, there is still much work to do on the spiritual path to live totally in this selfless domain. This becomes the ongoing work of a day-to-day spiritual practice.

Cultivating an active mindfulness of one's experience, moment to moment, is the path to awakening: taking a step, standing up, reaching for a door. When we're not mindful, different things happen. We can be going through the daily activities of life completely lost in thinking about the past or the future, about our hopes, our worries, our anxieties — without being present at all. On a somewhat more attentive level we may actually be present in our bodies, but still have the sense of "I'm standing up," "I'm sitting down," or "I'm doing this." Even though we're more present, we're still reinforcing the sense of someone solid and unchanging being there. On a deeper level of mindfulness, where our attention is very careful and deliberate, we begin to experience the reaching for a door, not as "I am reaching" but as a series of constantly changing sensations. Even in simple movements we can see so many things, so many different sensations coming and going — phenomena arising and passing — without adding the concept of self.

There are many ways to go about one's search for a personal relationship with the Dhamma. One traditional way is to leave the world and become a monk or a nun, to lead a life of renunciation such that one's lifestyle supports this experience of the deepest reality. However, this is not an option for most people.

A form that has evolved, which I think works well for many people, is the practice of intensive meditation retreats. People start with one weekend and then progress to retreats lasting from ten days to a month. During these retreats, people devote themselves full-time to intensive practice. Throughout the day they alternate between sitting and walking meditation. The intensity of the meditation is all that happens; there's no reading, no talking, no studying. It's all done in silence. In our fast-paced culture, a retreat provides a counterbalance to the rest of our lives and an opportunity to explore the usually unseen aspects of ourselves. It provides a space for us to develop, quite strongly, the power of the mind, the power of concentration. The challenge thus becomes one of learning how to integrate these two aspects of our lives: how to leave an intensive meditation retreat and carry the truth that we've seen inside ourselves into the business of our daily lives.

This integration is an ongoing process. Over and over we come on retreat, go deep in our practices, go back into the world, and explore how to integrate what we learned. Once or twice a year we go through this process. Over time the increased integration begins to happen and we begin to live it more and more deeply in our daily lives. This is how we make the Truth our own — by bringing it to life each day from our deepest experience of the Dhamma.

.IV.

Embracing God, Embracing Life

"An intense experience of mystery is what one has to regard as the ultimate religious experience."

— Joseph Campbell

The Power of Small Things

by SUE BENDER

❧

"Small miracles are all around us. We can find them
everywhere — in our home, in our daily activities,
and, where they are hardest to see, in ourselves."

I DIDN'T KNOW, WHEN I FIRST LOOKED AT AN AMISH QUILT and felt my heart pounding, that my soul was starving, that an inner voice was trying to make sense of my life. I just knew that the quilts seemed to reach out to me and say, "Sue, pay attention." My journey of the spirit began about twenty-five years ago, quite by accident. My husband and I had a summer home on Long Island. One day, I walked into a small men's clothing store and found these wondrous old Amish quilts on the wall. I was stunned.

I am an artist. I make hand-made, black-and-white pottery, and I was having my first big art show in New York City at the time. I was very busy; yet each day I found myself returning to that little shop to see the quilts. See-ing them touched something deep inside me. For the first time in my life, all my internal busyness stopped. All the fragments in my life — all the different, complex parts — became still and peaceful. That was the begin-ning of my spirit journey. Innocent enough.

I don't think of God with a capital G. My focus is on daily moment-to-moment living, which can, I believe, be a sacred spiritual experience. The outer form, the prac-tice, and the label may be different for each of us, but in a very deep and all-encompassing way I feel we are not alone. There is a *spirit*, a higher power — the *universe* — guiding us, leading us to what we are meant to learn and do — our destiny, our unique contribution to others.

After my first book, *Plain and Simple*, was published, I was surprised at first to receive many kind invitations to speak at churches, synagogues, and temples — Mormon, Episcopalian, Baptist, Jewish, Zen Buddhist. I first spoke at a First Presbyterian Church, where I asked the minister, "Why did you invite me to talk?"

"Because you are speaking about human values, and we all need to be reminded of human values," he answered.

His answer was a great gift. That's what I'm learning: to *remind* myself to see with fresh eyes the sacredness in everyday life. Small miracles are all around us. We can find them everywhere — in our home, in our daily activi-ties, and, where they are hardest to see, in ourselves.

Plain and Simple is about the time I spent with the Amish and what I learned from their simpler way of life.

Their life was a celebration of the ordinary. They valued work — all work. *How* they did things was as important as *what* they did.

I learned the power of having limits. The Amish have made one large choice. They lead a deeply religious life. Everything they do grows out of that choice. I was brought up to believe the more choices I had the better. But I was drowning in choices. There is a big difference between having lots of choices and *making* a choice. If you make a choice, you may have to eliminate certain things, but you can invest meaning in the things that remain. *To simplify, I have to say no,* I remind myself.

The Amish never preached to me. They never said, "Our way is better." They prayed for five minutes every morning and every evening. They spent the rest of their time living what they believed. Their life was all of one piece — all ordinary and all sacred. It became a wonderful model to aim for.

When I came home and tried to live what I had learned, it was harder than I expected. One day, I received a phone call that *Plain and Simple* had made the *New York Times* bestseller list. I was thrilled. That afternoon, I went to my local vegetable market and by chance bumped into a good friend. Beaming, I told her the remarkable news. She didn't even smile. Her first response was, "What number are you?" In that moment, I realized that we live in a world where nothing one does is ever enough.

"When will enough be enough," I began to ask myself.

When I began writing my book *Everyday Sacred*, I was filled with doubt. A critical voice inside me kept saying, "How dare you write a book with the word *sacred* in the title? You're not an expert!" Then I met Yvonne Rand, a wonderful, very wise Zen Buddhist priest. "You should be writing this book, not me," I said to her. "Sue," she responded in a thoughtful tone, "we can *both* write books. I can write one kind of book, but there are many, many people out there just like you — struggling to make every day count and wondering why they're never content." With that, I was able to relax and continue my work.

Soon after my conversation with Yvonne, an image of a monk's begging bowl came to me. I'm not a Buddhist, but I trusted that image of the begging bowl to guide me on my journey. I decided I would approach each day with my life an empty bowl. Each morning would bring a new, empty, fresh start. I would look at my ordinary life and do nothing differently, nothing at all, but instead simply examine what is there. I wouldn't try to become a great meditator or anything else. I'd just be myself.

This is when I began to understand that "God" or "spirit" is all around us. Our practice is to open our eyes and simply look around. For example, a wonderful man named Martin works in my favorite coffeehouse. No matter how long the line is, or how impatient the customers, he never loses his bearings. He never seems hurried or rushed. He performs his job with great care. Just at the last moment, as he prepares my cappuccino, he waves his hand, and, with a gentle flourish, creates a little smiling face in the foam. This, for me, is a sacred ritual. To notice these little everyday events is to notice the sacred — with a small s.

Wherever I go and whomever I speak to — a religious group, homemakers, artists, business people — I sense a hunger or a longing, even when people aren't sure what's missing in their lives.

Perhaps appreciating the beauty in everyday things, noticing the sacredness of everyday life, is something we need to cultivate in our lives. It requires some willingness, and a good deal of practice.

Don't think for a moment that I wake up every day, look around, and experience pure joy all the time — or that I'm always able to appreciate the small joys in life. I'm not. I'd like to be perfectly aware all the time, but I'm not. While writing *Everyday Sacred* I discovered I had a harsh, critical voice inside me. I had lived with it so long, I never noticed the influence it was having on my life. I not only listened to but believed what this "harsh judge" was saying. This voice passed judgment on everything I did.

Not everyone has a harsh judge, but many of us have some inner voice that has the power to undercut, to make us doubt ourselves, and to leave us wondering why we aren't more content. I realized it was important to find a different and kinder relationship with my judge because of its power to drain my positive energy. Learning to be more generous with ourselves is not selfishness. It is just the opposite: Trusting our own inner voice and needs helps us to be more truly generous with others.

One of the most important lessons I've learned has to

do with cracked pots. After admiring a friend's beautiful clay pot, I went to meet the wonderful man, Kevin, who made it. Often, just as Kevin was about to finish a pot, he would drop it and it would shatter. Eventually it dawned on him that he had a very destructive side — like my harsh judge! He decided to make a pot, consciously break it, and then piece it back together. Once he gave his "saboteur" a voice, he noticed he didn't ruin as many pots.

I took a workshop with Kevin. Right in the middle of it, he stopped and asked, "Would anyone like to crack their pot?" I raised my hand, picked one of my bowls, and then tried and tried to crack it on his cement floor. To my surprise, it was very difficult. I wouldn't let go! As in life, we say we want to change, but then we see how hard change is! You want to, but something holds you back. Finally, I let go and the bowl cracked in half. Then it was easy to crack the bowl into more pieces. As I collected them, Kevin came over and said, "Save the slivers!" He showed me how to reassemble the pieces of my cracked pot. I had to find two pieces that matched, like a jigsaw puzzle, and then, with shipbuilder's glue, hold the pieces very still for five minutes until they set. Piece by piece, my pot was put back together.

When I held the pieced-together pot in my hands, a circle was completed. It was remarkable. In the past, no matter what I did or accomplished, I still thought something was missing in my life, and never understood what it was. As I looked at the pot, I saw that nothing was missing. Nothing. I saw I was whole.

At that same moment, I realized this is true for each of us. We can spend our time and good energy focused on our imperfections, cracks, slivers, and flaws, or we can shift our perspective to see that those same qualities are what make us unique. My bowl was far more interesting than before it had cracked. And then I had one of those "Aha" moments. I saw, really saw, in every cell in my body:

To be *whole* doesn't mean we have to be perfect!

With that in mind, what really interests me is how we can bring spirit into form, how we can live our spirituality — not just talk about it or preach it, but really live it. How do you bring your spirit into your real life? How do you face your own little and big struggles?

When I started this journey, I was hoping for a *big* miracle, one that would change my life dramatically. What I found instead was far more useful — the extreme importance of *small* things. Maybe the most sacred things are the hardest to see because they are so obvious. My son David sends a weekly card to his 92-year-old grandmother. This is every bit as special as anything else he does. We all have our own version of David's card to his grandmother. Too often we take these small acts of kindness for granted. We think we have to offer others great achievements or gifts. Small acts of kindness make a difference — they have echoes out of proportion to the effort they take.

Often I remind myself of something that Mother Teresa said: "We do not do great things, we do only small things with great love."

Knowing that things I have learned from my own

struggles can be of use to others is deeply nourishing to me. Always striving for bigger, better, and more is, I believe, the disease of our culture. We set ourselves up to fail, which is a terrible waste of good energy and good spirit! When will enough be enough? I want to be able to say, "Who I am is enough. What I am doing right now is the best I can do — and it is enough!"

To me, success lies in looking at ourselves with "fresh eyes" — honoring ourselves and all the small steps and changes we make along the way. Out of that understanding we can honor others — just as they are.

The Community of God

by Rabbi Harold Kushner, Ph.D.

❧

"The first important element of a personal
relationship with God is a sense of humility."

I DEFINITELY BELIEVE IN A PERSONAL GOD, but I believe that
God is wholly other than you or me. Some forces in my
life, like gravity, are impersonal; they affect all of us the
same way. If you and I fall out of a window, we would fall
toward the pavement, accelerating at the same rate.
Other forces — love, courage, hunger — don't affect us
all the same way.

For me, God is personal in the sense that He affects
every individual differently. The rabbis of the Midrash
said, "God is like a mirror. The mirror never changes but
everyone who looks at it sees a different face."

I grew up in a moderately religious household. My
parents were very involved in our synagogue, and we went
to services constantly. For me, it became part of what I

did. Family came first and God was sort of an adjunct to that. God was the name we attached to the religious things we did as a family and as a community. So for me, religion begins not with a series of theological propositions, but with community. Religion is the articulation of the faith of perception, the view of purpose in life, the view of the world's holiness as articulated by a group.

Praying was as natural a part of growing up as was brushing my teeth. I learned the discipline of being grateful for all the things that happened in life — grateful for health and for the sunshine in the spring, grateful for recovery when I was sick, grateful for having parents who loved and protected me. This idea remained pretty much intact through my college education — with the usual adolescent skepticism — through my training to be a rabbi, and into my early years as a rabbi.

The crucial event in the development of my view of God came when my wife and I learned that our three-year-old son, Aaron, had a disease that would cause his death in his early teens. This contradicted everything my teachers had taught me about how the world worked, how God treated people. It forced me to abandon my idea that if I was a good and pious person, God would protect me and my family from tragedy and let it happen only to other people. I went through a difficult period of doubt, trying to figure out what God's relationship could possibly be to my son's illness. I was very angry at God. I felt I had kept my part of an implicit bargain and God had cheated and not kept His. But I didn't want to be angry at God and I didn't want to be estranged from God.

I was a person to whom religion and a sense of God's accessibility were extremely important. So I read everything I could about religion and the death of children, and in the Book of Job, especially in Archibald Mac-Leish's modern version, *J.B.*, I found an answer: the idea of "man forgiving God for the world's messiness and imperfection," the idea that God is not responsible for everything, but that some things in the world are beyond His power and that, as William Sloan Coffin said when his son died, "God's heart was the first to break." MacLeish's words enabled me to read the Book of Job in a totally new light, and I think that's when my awareness of the presence of God really started.

The conclusion I came to was that God does not send sickness or disease, accident or tragedy. These happen for other reasons — either from laws of nature or for reasons of human cruelty or foolishness. God sends the strength to survive and transcend the tragedy. God did not want my child to be sick and die, but God helped me face his illness with courage, and God gave me the insight to take this personal tragedy and forge it into an instrument of redemption that would help others. I learned to find God not in the tragedy, but in the capacity of the human soul to surmount and survive the tragedy. For me, that has been the source of my everyday experience with God. In the course of my work I visit people in hospitals and I walk away not asking the questions that someone else may ask — "Why does God permit cancer? Why does God permit Alzheimer's disease?" — but rather "Isn't it amazing that doctors and nurses could be so dedicated to trying to help people surmount illness?" For me, this is the presence of God in the hospital.

If we want to find God in Jewish tradition, we don't do it by turning our backs on the world and going into mystical contemplation. Psalm 146 begins implicitly by asking a theological question: "Where is God found?" Then it says, "God is the one who sustains the fallen and feeds the hungry and brings justice to the widow and the orphan." We find God by helping the poor, by providing homes for the homeless, by working for justice. And when we have done that, when we have done the sorts of things God stands for, we suddenly find that God has become present in our lives.

The first important element of a personal relationship with God is a sense of humility — a sense that letting God into our lives is not the result of our great achievements but of recognizing our limitations. If we're too full of ourselves, we leave no room for God. The Biblical definition of idol worship is not bowing down to statues, but worshipping the work of our own hands as the highest achievement and the highest source of value.

The second element is a sense of reverence, which we modern human beings have lost — a sense that there is something out there so much greater than ourselves that our human experience offers no metaphor, no analogy for. Part of reverence is the understanding that conversation with God involves listening much more than talking. Communicating with God is not an opportunity for us to tell Him things He would not otherwise know or to persuade Him of our merits. It's a matter of sharing our minds with Him so that His priorities and His way of seeing things enter into our minds. My teacher, Professor Abraham Joshua Heschel, said that prayer means learning to see the world from God's point of view.

A personal relationship with God enhances life. First, it enables us to accept our limitations without being frustrated by them. It assures us that problems we can't solve are not necessarily insoluble. Second, when we need it, God offers us a sense of forgiveness, a sense of cleansing from our incompleteness. We may have let Him down and disappointed Him, but we're still acceptable in His presence. When Jews gather for worship on Yom Kippur, The Day of Atonement, the first sentence of the liturgy is, "It is hereby decreed that it is permissible for sinners to be part of the congregation." It's precisely that message we're really coming for. Even if we did some things inadequately, we're still welcome to come into the sight of God. Last and perhaps most important, a personal relationship with God redeems us from the fear of death. We needn't be afraid that all our good deeds will vanish when we die.

I follow the work of Jewish theologian Martin Buber in that I believe God gives us the model of the I-Thou relationship. God never sees us in terms of what we can do for Him. He sees us in terms of how the relationship with Him can enhance our growth. And by that He teaches us how to model our relationships to our spouses, to our children, to our neighbors as I-Thou rather than on exploitative terms. We learn to relate to people toward the goal of mutual growth, not toward the goal of exploitation, advantage, or profit.

Jews tend to be uncomfortable speaking directly about God. Because they tend to find God manifest in relationships, they are likely to talk not so much about what God has meant in their lives, but about what other human beings as incarnations of God have meant in their lives — how, for example when they are depressed, when they are bereaved and grieving, God came to them in the incarnation of friends and neighbors who would not leave them alone. It's no fun to talk to a depressed person, and yet people found the energy and the need to do this because God was working through them. It is a Jewish affirmation that we see God in the lives and faces of all the people around us, so one of my congregants is more likely to say not that he found God in a moment of mystical insight, but that he found God when he felt terribly alone and somebody rang his doorbell and offered to sit with him and help him cry.

When people come to me and are devastated with a tragedy of some sort, the first thing I do is hug them and hold their hands, because the message I want to give is that I am there with them and that, as represented by my caring presence, God is there with them.

What I've learned is that "Why did this happen to me?" is not a question — it's a cry of pain. Persons who have suffered feel abandoned by God. For example, I have visited people dying of AIDS, and I discuss whether they feel they are dying without God — if they feel that God is punishing them for their homosexual activity or their drug use or whatever they think had given them the disease. Very often they do; and the one thing I can do is bring them some reassurance that God still cares for them. The most important message I give is that God did not want this to happen; God does not hate them. God, too, is grieving. I do this not with my theology, but with a sense of caring, with my handholding, with my willingness to sit and listen to their stories and feel with them.

What has held Judaism together for all these centuries and what I think really holds most religions together is the sense of community, of relationships — that we are a large family rather than a belief system. In Judaism, one leaves the Jewish people not when one stops believing in Jewish theology, but only when one no longer cares about the people. At a family picnic, for example, you can have a cousin who is the opposite of you in every way, and yet you know that person is your cousin. You can't find a thing that you agree on or have in common, but you know that you are linked by something much more permanent than political or literary opinion. That's the way Jews feel about one another.

When people ask me "Where is God?" I tell them I would rather rephrase the question to "*When* is God?" Encountering God is not a matter of being in the right place, but of doing the right thing. God comes into our lives when we do things that make us truly human. When we help the poor, when we speak out for justice, when we get over our exaggerated sense of our own importance, when we learn to respond with child-like awe to the sun shining in summer or to the snow falling in winter, when we get over being stuck on ourselves, we make room in our lives for God.

The Process of God

by ANNE WILSON SCHAEF, PH.D.

*"Trust the unfolding of your life and
see what you have to learn from that."*

GOD, TO ME, IS THE PROCESS OF THE UNIVERSE and probably beyond the universe — both separate from and yet one with all things. I believe that when we're living from our spirituality we are in harmony with and are one with that process. We affect that process and that process affects all of us when we are clear with ourselves and our personalities stay out of the way.

As a child, I was aware of the simplicity of my relationship with God. This relationship came from feeling close to and safe in nature. I lived near to the Cherokee Indians; my mother had been adopted into the Cherokee tribe. Much of my time was spent in the woods, really knowing the oneness of all things. My mother was aware of humanity's relationship with animals and nature, and how everything we did affected everything else. That connection was a big part of my spirituality, and it continues to be.

I grew up in the Bible Belt, and when very young I went to a Methodist church, usually with my mother. What I enjoyed was the church community, especially the hymn singing, the usual kind of Southern rip-snorter hymns. I went through many periods of questioning in high school and college, questioning what I had been taught, questioning the limitation of religions, seeing how the frequent rigidity of religion was different from what I had experienced in childhood as my relationship with God.

I still question how we see God, how we use God. Our society acts as if God is something that's carved in stone, making God static so that we feel more secure. I write a great deal about addictions, the addictive society, and addictive thinking models. When we are into our addictive process of thinking, we have an illusion of control. What we try to do is make the universe static so we feel "in control," or, more accurately, so we can maintain our illusion of control. We try to make our children static, our homes static. We think that if we can just get things the way we want them, we'll be safe, instead of taking the responsibility to learn about the dynamics of our process and live that process.

We've done the same thing with religion. We've taken the processes of some amazing people — great leaders and teachers — and have tried to make those processes static, teaching without understanding that it is the process of unfolding in the individual that gets to those teachings, to that understanding. We've taken the end-product of the process, but have forgotten it's through a dynamic evolution that we get to the end-product.

When I'm out of tune with the process, I experience a certain anxiety. I try to control myself and other people, to make things happen the way I think they should happen. When I'm in tune with the process and living out of it, I live a life of faith, and I trust my life as it unfolds.

For example, in my professional life there were periods when it became clear it was time for change. I had a large private practice, but over time I became increasingly aware that I was uncomfortable working with individuals in that setting. I was counting off the number of hours I had scheduled each day, and when someone terminated therapy, I didn't schedule someone new. After a while I asked myself, "What is happening here? Is it time for me to be doing something different?"

I had raised a family on my income from psychotherapy. My speaking engagements and workshops were frosting on the cake. I went into a panic. I thought, "If I don't see clients, how will I take care of my family?" Yet, my life was clearly showing me that I needed to take another path. So I took that leap of faith. I began conducting more trainings and workshops, doing more speaking engagements.

In the last few months it's become clear that again it is time to restructure the work I'm doing and move ahead to something else. But I don't plan my life. I don't say, "Well, now this is where it should go so I'm going to make this happen." It's never a problem when I trust the process and do whatever it is I need to do.

My work does not consist of trying to control others and teach them what to do. My work is to model. I believe that as people get in touch with themselves, they become more spiritual beings. Our addictive society and the addictive process — a layer over the living process that takes people away from their true selves — put people out of touch with their morality, their spirituality, their knowing their past. I work with people as they are, and I trust and facilitate while I encourage them to confront the addictive processes. As they deal with these addictive processes and try to live more with their living processes, the living processes increase and the addictive processes recede. They come to their own spirituality.

Our living process is our relationship with God. Regardless of what we have done, that process is there and is who we are. We must live more and more out of our faith. Some people translate this experience in a traditional Christian way, others in a traditional Buddhist way, and others view it as a higher power at work. However we live out our own spirituality is up to us.

I think the twelve-step program is the most effective tool for dealing with the addictive process. Part of that program is understanding that a power greater than ourselves can restore us to sanity. Step three in that program is turning over our lives and our will to that power. This "turning over" is a process every major world religion talks about.

One of my favorite quotes is from a black woman who

had been in twelve-step programs for a long time. She said, "Honey, even if you don't believe in God, can you believe you ain't Him?" I think that that is part of coming to know our own spirituality. It's beginning to recognize that we're not the center of the universe — that we are one with the universe and that we don't control it.

You are a process. The universe is a process. Everything around you is a process. Be in touch with that process and trust it. Trust the unfolding of your life and see what you have to learn from that.

Alive with God

by FATHER WILLIAM McNAMARA

"To be alive is to love. Those who live the most dangerously, creatively, and wonderfully are the great lovers in the world."

I AM THE DIRECTOR OF A CARMELITE HERMITAGE in Crestone, Colorado. Because we spend most of our time in solitude, our community life is very important. Some people misunderstand solitude and think of it as isolation. But it is exactly the opposite: if we really enter into genuine solitude, then we enter into the center of our being and connect with every other creature in the world. The communion achieved cannot be achieved in a crowd. When we emerge from that silence we really meet the other person, relate passionately and personally, and achieve presence. Therefore, the whole of spiritual life can be summed up in three words: personal, passionate, presence.

At our hermitage, the heart and center of all our practices, exercises, disciplines, and few rules relate significantly to being as constantly aware of God as we possibly can. The whole person is engaged in the single-hearted mindful presence of God: intellect, will, instincts, emotions.

But even in solitude, mindfulness doesn't come naturally. To attain mindfulness, I awake at four-thirty in the morning and begin to thank God for a new day, a new opportunity to discover Him, to enjoy Him in awe, to serve Him in awe; and then, by His power and grace, to be an instrument of His power and peace in my community and in the world. I am sure that the life of prayer and penance affects not only my immediate visible surroundings but worlds that I cannot dream of.

One of my favorite hermits, that great American author Henry David Thoreau, said that he would give first prize to the man who could live one day deliberately. That's what I mean by living mindfully. My early morning ethic is intended to achieve living one day deliberately — to become so centered that one becomes ultimately fascinated, ravished, and overwhelmed by the Mystery that permeates and suffuses all nature, all people, all reality.

One of the worst things we can do is slip or slide or drift into the day. It's important at the beginning of the day to think of ourselves as warriors and to engage in combat with the evils of the world, not merely to enjoy the day in a solipsistic way. Silence and solitude provide the best atmosphere for apocalyptic warfare with whatever evils dominate the world.

Genuinely religious people are not spooky, or bland, or stereotyped. They're simply more alive. Aliveness is primary. So is love. To be alive is to love. Those who live the most dangerously, creatively, and wonderfully are the great lovers in the world. The ultimate purpose of monastic life is to create an environment for lovers. One reason for being celibate is to be a greater lover. Although we have renounced certain genital aspects of sexuality, we have not repressed our sexuality, but refined and empowered that energy into creative aspects and expressions of love of another kind. The only reason to renounce one particular pleasure is to enjoy the unbearable pleasure of God's company.

When I go to the city, people ask me, "What's it like to get back to the real world?" I say, "Where? I just left it." I even hate to distinguish between a profane world and a sacred world. There's only one world. There are degrees and layers of reality in that one world. The closer we come to the center, to the heart of things, the more we find God. If I come to the heart of a human meeting, if I come to the heart of a beautiful woman, if I come to the heart of a dog, I meet God. God's at the heart of everything.

We must get off the surface, away from the periphery, and move into the center where the fire is, and there become consumed by the fire and really become alive. Aliveness is the first effect of living a disciplined life. We must all become disciplined wild people. That's the spiritual life. You participate in the life of the spirit — the spirit of God. God has no boundaries and no limitations.

He's infinitely wild! All the psychiatrists and psychologists I know agree that one of the major reasons most people have mental problems is that they are not wild enough. Their lives have been too restricted and too tame. In the wilderness we try to participate in the wildness of God, not by developing multiple, dissipated, unconnected passions and desires, but by having one governing passion and desire that gathers all our little desires into one single-hearted mindful aim: realized union with God, a deeply personal, passionate relationship with the living God.

There are three steps in cultivating a relationship with God: meditation, prayer, and contemplation. Meditation — what you do, the way you think, the way you read — leads you to prayer. You must take a segment of the day when you stop all the ordinary aspects of your life and enter into a silent, solitary sphere of being. There you begin to meditate. St. Teresa defined meditation as a heart-to-heart conversation with God, our Father, who we know loves us. To be known, to be loved — that's what people need in meditation.

If you are led to prayer, the second step, then you cease to be the primary actor in this relationship and become wisely passive. Then meditation turns into prayer and you talk to God.

Prayer is a cry of the heart. Your ideas sink into your heart and the heart catches fire. You cry from out of your own inner truth. Sometimes that cry is exultation, sometimes sorrow, sometimes grief, sometimes madness — but always a cry of the heart. Now God becomes the primary active one. You are overwhelmed by the power of God, the spirit of God; and you are turned into a contemporary Christ. You think like Christ, you love like Christ, you act like Christ. That's prayer: simply to be there.

Then comes the final stage: contemplation — when you simply rest. The great scholastic theologians describe contemplation as the pure intuition of God born of love. When you have reached this point, you have nothing to say, nothing more to do. You are simply caught up in love, overwhelmed by being loved. If you really contemplate, your efforts will be effective and enduring.

Action without contemplation is blind. I am particularly critical of this situation in politics and universities today. During their college years, most people lose their relationship with God. They lose their faith, humanity, and sanity because they're overwhelmed by data and information, but never achieve an understanding or wisdom, never move into the Mystery. Life becomes a series of problems to be solved instead of the Mystery to be lived. Very few take that crucial segment of the day when they do nothing but enter the chamber of love and let God reveal Himself and then send them, imbued with His power and His fire and His love, back into the marketplace — but transfigured: glowing and shining with the incandescent light of the spirit.

God is surprise. He always takes us by surprise! He is nothing like we imagine. God transforms us in ways we never dreamt of. One nun came from Florida during the rainy season to make her retreat. She wanted to intensify the pious routine she was already in — when this routine was the greatest enemy of her transformation. She wanted more pious reading, more dialoguing, more meditating.

We met her at the airport, then traveled on our dirt road in a tractor, hauling her in an open cart thirty-five miles into the woods in the pouring rain! She stayed a month and said that her religious experience was not the reading, not the meditation, not the dialogue, not what she planned on, but her soaking-wet tractor ride! That's how God works. He comes and goes as He will.

God is not nice, God is not a mascot, God is not an uncle. God is an earthquake. If we're going to enter His cave, we're entering into the presence of a lion. Who knows if we're going to come out alive? God is love, all right. But because His love is unlimited and boundless; it's fierce! We can't afford to be routine or trivial about it. We can't afford to reduce God to our own measure and our own management. We can't possess God or cope with Him the way we want. We must be overwhelmed by the leonine surprise of His personal passionate presence.

.V.

God in Everyday Life

"True religion is real living; living with all one's soul, with all one's goodness and righteousness."

— Albert Einstein

Life as God

by SHAKTI GAWAIN

*"In our society we have created a sedentary lifestyle,
which may be one reason we are so spiritually deprived."*

GOD IS THE LIFE FORCE THAT CREATES EVERYTHING —
including us — continues to flow through us, and
keeps us alive. That life force contains total wisdom and
power. The degree that we attune ourselves to it and are
able simply to move with it and trust it is the degree to
which we find ourselves in a personal relationship with
God. I believe we all have the source of truth, the connection to the deepest truth within ourselves, and that we
can connect with it by learning to listen to our intuition,
to ask for that deepest truth, and to trust and be willing to
act on it moment by moment in our lives.

I was not born or raised with this belief. I was brought
up in an intellectual, educated, rational, nonreligious
family. I distinctly remember when I was young feeling

that God was an idea people made up to make themselves feel better because they really didn't know the answers to most of life's profound questions: Why are we here? How did we get here? What's going on? I believed that religion and spiritual things were basically superstitions, and that if something couldn't be proved scientifically, it didn't exist.

Then, when I was in college, I began to have experiences that opened me a little more to the other feelings and taught me to trust in the moment and in myself — that is, my intuition, my inner guidance.

After college I traveled around the world. I didn't know where I was going or what I was going to do, and I didn't have much money. That journey was a metaphysical opening for me. As I trusted the spirit within me, I found that I was taken care of and that things worked out for me. By the time I got to India, I had almost no possessions, but it was an extremely liberating experience for me. Somewhere along the way I had found a deep connection to the spirit.

I had a mystical experience with the God Shiva while I was on a boat on the Ganges River, the holy river in India, and felt I experienced the energy of Shiva. In Indian religion, there's the God Brahma, who is the creator; the God Vishnu, who is the preserver; and the God Shiva, who is the destroyer. Shiva represents the principle that life is constant change and that we must always release the old and open to the new. We must be willing to constantly change. Shiva is the lord of the dance, and they say his dance keeps the universe in motion.

By the time I came back to this country, I knew that I wanted to pursue consciousness — whatever that was — and my personal growth. I started reading books and going to many spiritual teachers and psychological growth workshops. Ken Keyes's Living Love Center was an important influence, and reading some of the Seth material had a profound influence on me. *The Nature of Personal Reality* opened me to the idea that we are spiritual beings who are creating our own reality here.

I said to myself: "If I'm creating my own reality, then I would like to start shaping my life more the way I want it to be and live less haphazardly." I started to use techniques of creative visualization and affirmation. I found that using these techniques changed my life dramatically, and I wanted to show them to other people. I began leading workshops; then I wrote *Creative Visualization*.

Until that time, on certain subtle levels I had always felt like a victim of life, as if life is something that happens to us and all we can do is make the best of it. Now I began to understand that we in fact do create our own reality, which puts the power right in our own hands. Nobody is doing this to us — we're doing it, we're creating it, and we can create it however we want it.

Believing that I am a creative channel for the power of the universe was a big shift for me. I started taking complete responsibility for my life, creating it moment by moment. I eventually began to realize it wasn't really myself creating, but a higher power that is in everything in the universe, that creates everything, and that comes through me (although I have some ability to channel or guide it by blocking it or allowing it to come through). And I realized I can filter it and dilute its creative power, or I can work to release my filters and become a more powerful channel.

My spiritual practice became one of surrendering to that deeper, wiser, more powerful force within myself. Rather than thinking so much about manipulating my life, I began to shift my focus and ask, "How can I align myself with my own deepest wisdom? How can I align my personality self, which often is somewhat confused and unclear, surrender it to the deepest knowing part of myself, and allow that to take me where I truly want to go?"

I've come to a point where I have a profound trust in my inner guidance. I'm not always able to reach it because of human confusion, old emotional pain and patterns, and situations I must work through. But increasingly I'm able to feel, listen to, and experience that deep sense of truth and knowingness. It's an unmistakable feeling of great love and power coming through me.

That has been my personal relationship with God — a connection with the powerful, loving, wise energy in all of us, in all creation. It *is* the life force itself. We can all have contact with it each moment in our lives, but it takes commitment and practice. We must be willing to move through all our deepest fears, doubts, and misunderstandings.

Most religions and spiritual paths give us a lot of rules and structure, which, at a certain stage in our development, we need, just as little children need some rules to make their way through life safely. At some point, however, we must let go of those rules and travel another path with a different set of rules that open us to another aspect of God or of ourselves. Gradually, we must come to a place of our personal relationship with God that is beyond all rules and all dogma.

To me, the function of a good spiritual path, teacher, therapist, healer, or helper is to support people in trusting themselves and their personal connections with the higher power. When we find our connections there aren't anymore rules, because life is a changing, spontaneous, ever-evolving experience. If we try to hold onto what worked for us last year or last week or even a minute ago, we get into trouble. Life is always challenging us to develop new aspects of ourselves and develop trust in new ways. If we try to hold onto rules, we block ourselves and stop the progress. But if we use the rules for as long as they serve us and then release them when appropriate, if we keep asking for guidance, then we can keep changing and growing. We all have our own paths that in some ways are different from everyone else's, yet we need to share our experiences and give each other support and encouragement.

I have always found that my physical body is one of the most important ways that I connect with spirit. Our world is presently evolving into a higher level of consciousness, and it's especially important for us to recognize that God is the life force in the earth, in the other beings around us, and in our bodies. The personal experience of God, I'm beginning to realize, is the experience of ecstasy in our physical bodies.

Earlier in my life, mind-expanding drugs helped me to know that there *was* that kind of an experience. But drugs are a trap; bliss must be found through natural means, through whatever allows us to feel the life force flowing through our bodies. Bodies love to move; they love to be active. In our society we have created a sedentary lifestyle, which may be one reason why we are so spiritually deprived. We've lost that natural, blissful connection that happens when the body is moving with the life force through working, dancing, or any natural movement.

Acknowledging our bodies is the opposite of what some traditional spiritual paths have taught us: that the body is a distraction from spirit and that we must transcend it. But I feel that the physical plane is a particularly exciting and challenging place to be. I think we have chosen to be here to develop another level of our Godselves in the physical form. As long as we have taken that challenge, then, let's go ahead and do it! Let's stop trying to get away from our bodies, when the point is to get *into* them and to experience how exquisitely pleasurable life in a physical form is meant to be.

To me, spiritual energy is the same as the life force. Our spiritual energy is completely and intimately connected with our sexual energy, which is connected with our hearts and our love and the life force. Being able to express our love sexually is probably one of the highest experiences of God there is, because it's the only experience that can take us through all our deepest, darkest places into the total fullness of who we are. Unfortunately, this is extremely complicated for us; we have emotional patterns we need to work out before we're able to experience sexual love fully.

Another important physical connection to God is through the earth — another manifestation of our physical form, the mother of all our physical forms. Connect with the earth. Find some place that's very beautiful to you (it could be the park across the street, the beach, the woods) and spend some time there without distractions. Lie down and look at the clouds above you. It can be very powerful to feel your body against the earth, to feel the energy of the earth connecting with your body. Stand next to a tree and put your hands on it, or hug it and feel the energy of the tree and your body's energy as they connect. Anything that helps you connect with your body and the physical earth will also be that connection to the creative life force.

The Peace of the Divine Reality

by THICH NHAT HANH

"When I have a toothache, I discover that not having a toothache is a wonderful thing. That is peace."

I WOULD LIKE TO SHARE A POEM WITH YOU, written by a friend who died at the age of twenty-eight in Saigon, about thirty years ago. After he died, people found many beautiful poems he had written, and I was startled when I read this poem:

> *Standing quietly by the fence,*
> *you smile your wondrous smile.*
> *I am speechless, and my senses are filled*
> *by the sounds of your beautiful song,*
> *Beginningless and endless.*
> *I bow deeply to you.*

"You" refers to a flower, a dahlia. That morning as he passed by a fence, he saw that little flower very deeply, and, struck by the sight of it, he stopped and wrote that poem.

I enjoy this poem very much. You may think that the poet was a Zen master, because his way of looking and seeing things is very deep. But he was just an ordinary person, a poet. I don't exactly know how or why he was able to see like that, but it is exactly the way we practice Buddhist meditation, the practice of mindfulness. We try to be in touch with life in the present moment and look deeply into the things that happen to us in the present moment. We do that while we drink tea, while we walk, sit down, and so on. The secret of the success is that you are yourself, you are really yourself, and when you are really yourself, you can encounter life in the present moment.

During his Last Supper, Jesus Christ told his disciples: "This piece of bread is my flesh. Eat it." That was a radical statement. He must have noticed that his twelve friends were not awake, and when he saw that, he wanted to say something strong to wake them up, to help them live fully in the present moment. He also told them, "This wine is my blood. Drink it." Eating bread and really eating the bread, drinking wine and really drinking the wine, looking at a flower, looking at the eyes of a child, at the Kingdom of God, at the Pure Land, is right here.

There is another story about a flower, a story well known in Zen circles. One day the Buddha held up a flower in front of an audience of 1,250 monks. He did not say anything for quite a long time. Suddenly, he smiled. He smiled because someone in the audience smiled at him and at the flower. The name of that monk was

Mahakashyapa. Only one person smiled, and the Buddha smiled back and said, "I have a treasure of insight, and I have transmitted it to Mahakashyapa." That story has been discussed by many generations of Buddhists, and people continue to look for its meaning. To me the meaning is quite simple. When someone holds up a flower and shows it to you, he wants you to see it. And if you keep thinking, you miss the flower. The person who is not thinking, who was just himself, was able to encounter the flower in depth, and he smiled.

That is the problem with life. If we are not here, if we are not in the present moment, fully ourselves, we miss everything. When a child presents himself to you, with his smile, and if you are not really there, you are thinking about the future or you are thinking about the past, or you are preoccupied by other problems, then the child is not really there for you. The technique of being alive, of living in the divine and earthly realities simultaneously, is to go back to yourself. Then the child will appear like a marvelous reality; then you can see her smile and embrace her.

Living in this marvelous reality, living in peace, is something we all want. But I would like to ask: Do we have the capacity of enjoying peace? If peace is there, will we be able to enjoy it, or will we find it boring? To me, peace and happiness and joy and life go together, and we can experience the peace of the divine reality right in the present moment. It is available, inside us and around us. If we are not able to enjoy that peace, how can we make peace grow?

When I have a toothache, I discover that not having a toothache is a wonderful thing. That is peace. I had to have a toothache in order to be enlightened, to know that not having one is wonderful. My nontoothache is peace, is joy. But when I do not have a toothache, I do not seem to be very happy. Therefore, to look deeply at the present moment and see that I have a nontoothache, that can make me very happy already.

I know a doctor who lost her eyesight because during the night, she used the wrong eye drops, and a few months later, she was not able to see anything. Every time she wants to remember the lines on her son's face, she has to call him close to her and rediscover those lines with her fingertips. To her, to be able to see things would be a miracle. She says that she would be in paradise if she could recover her eyesight. According to that criterion, most of us are already in paradise, because we have eyes capable of seeing. If we open our eyes we can see the blue sky, the white clouds, the clear stream, the flowers, the beautiful child. We need only to be mindful that we have eyes, and they can make us very happy. An element of peace is already here.

There are so many things that can provide us with peace. Next time you take a shower or a bath, I suggest you hold your big toes in mindfulness. We pay attention to everything except our toes. When we hold our toes in mindfulness and smile at them, we will find that our bodies have been very kind to us. We know that any cell in our toes can turn cancerous, but our toes have been behaving very well, avoiding that kind of problem. Yet, we have not been nice to them at all. These kinds of practices can bring us happiness.

When we contemplate the body in the body, we can discover these kinds of things. When we contemplate the feelings in the feelings, we discover there are many beautiful seeds of feelings in us. We can help ourselves to happiness and joy, because if we do not, we shall be in touch only with the painful aspects of life. We usually ask, "What is wrong?" and focus all our energy and attention on that while our happiness grows thinner and thinner. We neglect what is right, what is wonderful in us and around us. The practice of mindfulness of what is *not* wrong is wonderful.

We were able to smile a lot when we were young, but life is so hard that when we grow up, we hardly smile. I know people who have not smiled for ten or twenty years. The seeds of the smiles in the depths of their consciousness have not had a chance to arise for a long time. They only ask, "What is wrong?" So, asking the questions, "What is right? What is not wrong?" is a good beginning. By asking in this way and paying attention to these fresh elements that are healing and refreshing, we are able to heal ourselves, to grow, and to generate joy and happiness for our sake and for the sake of people who live around us.

The Buddha delivered a sermon on the mindfulness of breathing. He proposed sixteen exercises for us to practice. These exercises are wonderful. The first exercise is so simple: "Breathing in, I know that I am breathing in. Breathing out, I know that I am breathing out."

Just that. If you find these sentences too long, you can say just two words: "in, out." You breathe in and you know it is an in-breath, and you breathe out and say, "out," recognizing it as an out-breath. That is all.

I think Mahakashyapa was practicing this mindfulness when the Buddha held up the flower, and that is why the encounter between him and the flower was possible. All the others were thinking, and their thinking blocked the encounter. Thinking is important, but but most of our thinking is useless. It seems that we have cassette tapes in our heads, always running, day and night. We think of this and we think of that, and it is difficult for us to stop. With a cassette, we can just press the Stop button. But with our thinking, we do not have such a button. So when we think too much, we worry, we cannot sleep, we block our encounters with the present moment.

According to this method of breathing, when we breathe in and out, we stop thinking, because "in, out" are not thoughts — they're only words that help us concentrate on our breathing. If we keep breathing in and out and smiling for a few minutes, we become quite refreshed. We recover ourselves, and then we can encounter the flower, the piece of bread, the wine, the child. We do not miss anything that is happening in the present moment.

Breathing in and out is very important, and it is enjoyable! You know, when you have a stuffed nose, you cannot enjoy breathing. When you have asthma, you cannot enjoy breathing. But when the air is clean and you do not have asthma, it is wonderful to breathe. To me, breathing is a joy that I cannot miss. Every day I practice breathing, and in my small meditation room is this sentence: "Breathe, you are alive!" Just breathing and smiling can make us very happy, and when we breathe consciously we recover ourselves completely and encounter life in the present moment. To me, this is the Kingdom of Heaven. The real miracle is not to walk on water, but to walk on the earth, to be alive in the present moment. If we live in mindfulness, it is possible to encounter God right in the present moment while we are washing the dishes, looking at a flower, looking in the eyes of a child.

When we are in touch with refreshing, peaceful, and healing elements within ourselves and around us, we learn how to cherish and protect these things and to make them grow. These are the elements of peace and happiness available to us anytime. If we do not look closely at these simple things, we may find them boring.

There are people who cannot enjoy simple pleasures, and that is why they seek drugs, alcohol, sexual misconduct, and many other things that destroy them, their bodies, their minds, and their families, and cause their children and grandchildren to suffer. If we educate ourselves and our children on how to enjoy peace in the present moment and to be happy with the refreshing and healing elements that are available, we will avoid these kinds of traps. Life can be found only in the present moment. The past is gone, the future is not yet here, and if we do not go back to ourselves in the present moment, we cannot be in touch with life.

Who Speaks?

by MARSHA SINETAR

❧

*"Only love heals, makes whole, takes us beyond
ourselves. . . . Love gets us There, lets us know Who speaks."*

CHILDHOOD WAS LARGE MINDED. My family was intelligent, intensely creative, had a lively humor and good, firm moral tone. Ours was not a typically religious nest. Dogma, "religiosity" — any legitimized, organized specialness — was felt too restrictive a thought system to house the mind and style in which my parents lived.

In particular, when it came to me and God, my father consciously, philosophically restrained his charismatic influence. He expected me to use my mind to ask and answer for myself life's big questions. I tried to look and listen deeply — as substantively as a four or five year old could. My childhood's key and central question was, "Who speaks?"

My grandmother was an active spiritual instigator.

She stimulated what she called spiritual precociousness. She conspired with me. No doubt against my father's careful planning, she taught me as much as she knew about God from the viewpoint of the world's formalized religions. Mostly on the sly, we two renegades routinely slipped away to cross-cultural worship. My grandmother was a true ecumenical master; we made all the rounds. With her smallish, wrinkled hand clamped around my even-smaller, lineless one, she regularly escorted me to Buddhist and Hindu temples, to synagogues — especially on High Holy Days, which she loved — and to cathedrals, which I loved. God's living, active presence was there for me. The services, the liturgy, the prayers — even the architecture — shimmered. I felt that God lived in a nice house. I also knew He lived in me and in every devotee; I thought He absolutely undergirded all humanity with evidential Oneness. Those were bright, free-thinking days.

Such experiences, and others that I courted on my own, richly fed my inherent spiritual appetite. But years passed — dark, difficult ones — before I was satiated by the simple act of giving myself over to what I knew to be a radical interior summons. Today I have full confidence in this holy writ, with faith in its corresponding requisite of unconditional surrender. I regularly face what pop-psychology now terms "letting go." This movement, this ruination of habit, mind, and comfort simultaneously disorients and unsettles me while it integrates my whole being and my life.

However, before being strengthened by the organizing principle within that special disharmony, first I was significantly weakened by painful loss, the uprooting and dissolution of my small family, and economic hardship. Of course, given severe childhood losses, my first loyalties went to the world, to its securities and applause. No one could have accused me of any incapacity to "enjoy life" as convention defines that phrase.

Yet, as I came to — or rather transcended — my senses, St. Augustine's *Confessions* guided me to sanity. This autobiography of the prodigal son's return validated what I well knew but temporarily had rejected: Augustine's tumultuous youth, his description of his "great perverseness," his stunning realization that without God he could find no rest, no true interior pace, reassured and led me. For this was my experience, my own life's motif. So somewhere around this time I bit the bullet and marched myself to St. Michael's Church and asked to be baptized a Christian. This adult choice, this first legitimate commitment, made all the difference; it ignited its own spirited harvest.

This, then, the truthful acknowledgment and hesitating obedience to my life's disruptive but authentic call, has become a benchmark of what I now trust. For me, relinquishment, "letting go," has required — has built — my faith. Submission to the truth in faith comes by virtue of a grace. This regenerates, recreates, and feeds a life. Grace stirs us up. It makes us yearn for rearrangement, reach for reconfiguration and a truthful life. In faith we lose dishonesties, weaknesses, and subtle self-betrayals that we previously chose.

As we in faith (and I may add utter vulnerability)

obey this impulse, this movement of our souls, we gain the courage to be, we somehow are made able to embrace the void. Ironically, just as we gain this courage to be, the void somehow erases personal being, makes us nothing, deletes us.

I am not one to tell anyone specifically "how" to proceed or to say exactly what happens — what phrases or experiences or bright celestial sounds or pain to expect. My foolish notion is that those who direct us too exactly based on what has happened to them rob us of surprise and wonder, restrict us by their frames. In our desperation, we often guiltily collude. No matter. This, too, passes. For the Lord "comes as a thief in the night."

Each spiritual tradition gives different keys for our unique passage. Zen, Yoga, the Sufis, shamanism, classical Judeo-Christian chants, prayers, and rituals unearth us in their own ways. Sufi literature, for instance, provides novel ingress. Whirling dances bring aspirants to so joyful and self-forgetful a state that, ecstatically, they tear off clothes, cry out, become the void. But Sri Ramana Maharshi taught that simple being is enough.

All prayer seems to be our cry for access, our attempt in word or deed to touch God's hem. Whether we are feeling or cool and cerebral, whether we prefer to concentrate on form or practice negating all form or work toward self-surrender must matter less than that we choose strongly for a way that permits love, brings us to a worldless, wordless core within that *is* peace, *is* radiance, *is* that mystical union about which saints embody in their lives. A reader once sent me these tender lines from

Deuteronomy: "The eternal God is a dwelling place, and underneath are the everlasting arms." What could be clearer? What do we wait for? St. Therese of Lisieux instructed us further: "[Happiness] is not what attracts me.... It's Love! To love, to be loved, and to return to the earth to make love loved."

Only love heals, makes whole, takes us beyond ourselves. Love — not necessarily mushy sentiment or docile passivity — is both right motive and right result. Love gets us There, lets us know Who speaks.

At one extreme, many people completely shy away from freedom. Instead, angrily I think, they cling to rules, intellectualize, honor convention more than God's spontaneous open love. Less extreme, most of us also postpone our true good, sensing that we must live in wilderness, in unfamiliar territory — Reality. But whether by emotionless, incremental entry or by cataclysmic, high feeling, surely we can simply learn to *be* as God simply is. For haven't we been especially invited — by birth and by His creation — specifically addressed?

Sometimes addressed personally, we stumble "in," without desire, device, or premeditation. While fishing, doing the laundry, fixing a car motor, in prayer or meditation, we, too, through unmerited favor, can be reborn.

How can anyone not be touched or moved — forever changed — by God's grand, timeless creations? In nature, surrounded by pure, immortal, elemental beauty we rejoin that which is eternal, that which always is. By prayer, reading scriptures, through concentrated, devoted work or selfless service or simply by living life, we can recover life. This is healing rebirth. Formal theologies, myths, poetry, music, art, dance, and our own instinctive, primal intuition spark it. God's "everlasting arms" are closer to us than we are to ourselves, yet more and yet beyond.

John Muir, an uncommon saint in his own right, wrote that he wanted to spend all his time in an idle manner, "literally gaping with all the mouths of soul and body, demanding nothing, fearing nothing, but . . . hoping and enjoying tremendously." This transcendental daydreaming, Muir felt, was the only valid business of life. This is my favored way.

I have a special call and disposition for silence. But I know that to some, quiet is pointless. After all, what can you do without talking? Well, plenty. More important is what happens to you in silence. It is a perfect replica of inmost poverty. Periods of silence regenerate, simplify, and organize my life. Silence has strengthened my good will, brought peace of mind, produced for me a new life — *nova creatura.*

Not for an instant do I prescribe this as a method for others or for what is popularly called "self-discovery." Silence is severe, a discipline with special rules and dangers. If we practice to avoid, to mire in self-centeredness, we are done in. When we practice correctly, the fruits of silence are the fruits of the spirit: joy, peace, faithfulness, self-control, love. Approval-seeking weaknesses, the world's noise and its hopeless reality fade. Perhaps this is why a Jewish proverb teaches that silence heals all ailments. Silence teaches love, makes us able to receive love and to extend it, yet in our own authentic, proper way. This means we will love differently than the world expects — we will surprise and often disappoint.

No one writes more eloquently of silence than Thomas Merton. He has been a distant, if also absent, teacher. He says for me what I am too dull to say alone: "Let me seek then, the gift of silence . . . where everything I touch is turned into prayer; where the sky is my prayer, the birds are my prayer, the wind in the trees is my prayer, for God is all in all."

In truth, my life is very ordinary and specific — not problem-free, abstract, or theoretical. I love the wood-carrying, bird-feeding, floor-washing, bed-making, cooking, showering, coffee-klatching times. Friends and neighbors to whom I turn for talk, advice, and help — practical, useful acts and useless ones as well — these make up my life.

Too much talk of mystic things, like voids and transcendences, makes me nervous, misses the point — probably even makes God edgy. Down-to-earth, physical, relational, and quite creaturely realities (and not all beautiful, either) also shape and bless us. Surely these, too, point to God, permit dialogue and insight. Surely these lend life its worth and flavor. These, to me, seem holy, purposeful reminders that Who speaks is God, in whom we dwell, whose living presence addresses us to "make love loved."

Encountering God

by HUSTON SMITH, PH.D.

❧

*"People are of different spiritual temperaments
and therefore will approach God in different ways."*

I MUST CONFESS that the prospect of sharing what it's like
to have a day-to-day, moment-to-moment, personal relationship with God made me apprehensive. Why? Was it
the presumption that I have a moment-to-moment relationship with God — one that I am consciously aware of?
Or was my reluctance one of good taste, the issue of
whether it's appropriate to parade intimacies in public?
Underlying these doubts was the question of whether I
know what my relationship to God is. The arrangement
feels more like a mystery out of which my life is lived,
rather than a relationship that is open to my conscious
awareness and direct inspection.

In the end, though, the premise that prompted this
book — that we can learn from one another on this

matter — prevailed.

When, on the National Broadcasting Company's *Wisdom* series I asked Daisetz Suzuki if he was born with a religious impulse, he answered, "Not born, but it awakened."

"When did it awaken in you?" I wanted to know.

"Well, I do not know exactly. But the starting point was marked, perhaps, when I was 16 or 17 I wanted to get my religious yearnings somehow settled."

I could have answered the same: the deepest yearnings of which I am consciously aware have always been religious. I consider the religious impulse to be part of the human makeup; the search for cosmic understanding is as much a part of the religious impulse as is the search for cosmic belonging. In my case, though, early conditioning doubtless contributed to the strength of the drive, for my parents were missionaries in China and I grew up in a devoutly religious home.

Because we were the only Westerners in our small Chinese town, I was imprinted by my parental role models. When I came to America for college I assumed that it was to obtain credentials for returning to China as a missionary in my own right. The dynamism of the West soon changed that prospect, however. Central Methodist College boasted only six hundred students, and the population of Fayette, Missouri, was less than three thousand, but compared with small-town China it was exciting to the point of extinguishing all thoughts of returning to the Orient. My religious impulse remained intact, however, so I decided that instead of being a missionary I would be a minister.

A second vocational shift occurred during my junior year in college, when the intellect became real for me. A brilliant and charismatic philosophy professor deserves much of the credit, but I can actually date the night the conversion occurred. During a meeting of our philosophy club my excitement had been mounting all evening, and as we walked back to our dormitory my mind seemed to explode from within. Old walls were shattered, and beyond them there was nothing between me and the Infinite. I wonder if I slept at all that night. I would not have recognized the words then, but that night I discovered I was a *jnana yogin*, one whose primary approach to God is through knowledge (more on this point later). Almost at once I shifted my vocational plans toward teaching.

The intellectual excitement I felt continued during my graduate years at the University of Chicago, but my work there in philosophy and religion focused, as had my undergraduate program, exclusively on the West, so it was only after I started teaching that I discovered that spiritual wisdom was not a Western monopoly. This occurred first through the writings and then through the friendship of Gerald Heard and his intellectual partner, Aldous Huxley. I discovered the mystics, and because the mystics speak a universal language, their writings led me successively through the Vendanta, Buddhism, and Sufism, spending roughly a decade at each stop. At no point on this journey did I feel that I was leaving anything behind, least of all Christianity, for after Asia had opened my eyes I discovered there were Jewish and Christian mystics, too. My pilgrimage simply confirmed the same essential truths by revealing them in different idioms.

My relationship with God through my mid-twenties was cast in a Protestant, pietistic mold wherein God was approached through a personal, love-and-service relationship with Christ. I continue to honor that mode and to work on it in part. But, in addition, the Hindu doctrine of the four yogas — the notion that people are of different spiritual temperaments and therefore will approach God in different ways: *jnanis* through knowledge, *bhaktis* through love, *karmic* types through service, and *rajic* types through meditation — freed me to see that there were other channels through which spiritual energies may flow. My personal relationship with Christ, though real, was not very intense, whereas *thoughts* of God could hold me spellbound for an entire night.

Such jnanic knowledge is apt to be misunderstood by those who have not experienced it — by those whose yogic strengths lie elsewhere. It has nothing to do with quantity of information or logical dexterity. It is rather that thoughts, for the jnanic, possess a body of sorts, a three-dimensional substantiality that makes thoughts real in ways they are not for other people. Plato's ideas, for example — the Good, the True, and the Beautiful — for the jnanic (or gnostics, as they might be called in the West if that word is distinguished from gnosticism) are not the empty abstractions that others take them for. They are almost palpably real. And their reality excites; they all but dance and sing. This distinguishes the *theoria* that discusses them from theories as these typically function in science. The Greek word *theoria* derived from the theater, which makes jnanic knowledge closer to vision than to thought as we usually use the word. It is seeing, albeit with the eye of the soul. And the vision attracts. Aristotle compounded Goodness, Truth, and Beauty into his Unmoved Mover, which moves the entire universe by force of attraction. But my point is that ideas attract jnanis, who are drawn to ideas because they love them — and we are drawn to and become like that which we love. Socrates said that to know the good is to do it. Saint Paul disagreed, but he was a different temperamental type — a bhakti rather than a jnani yogin — so knowing was not the same for the two men.

This all relates to God, for though I have not used the word, I have been speaking of nothing else. God is the Good, the True, the Beautiful — and Power and Mystery, we should add — fused so completely that the five are not five but one. In my best moments I am drawn to that God as moth to flame, and at such times I do not know whether my happiness is the rarest or the commonest thing on earth, for all earthly things seem to reflect it. But I cannot hold onto it. When those grace-filled moments arrive, it does not seem strange to be so happy, but in retrospect I wonder how such gold of Eden could have been mine.

It is easy to make much of direct mystical disclosures. Desert stretches provide opportunities for growth that are as important as mountaintop experiences, and theologians assure us that souls can be established in an abiding relationship with God without being sensibly aware of God's presence. The goal is not altered states by altered traits. Aldous Huxley's observation that the task of life is to overcome the fundamental human disability of egoism comes in here, for every step we take in overcoming that is in God's direction.

Walking Home

by HUGH PRATHER

❧

"No matter how far I strayed in my life ... my yearning
for God has always gently lifted me from whatever
destructive path I was on."

WHEN I WAS GROWING UP, my family used a Christian Science practitioner by the name of Mrs. Fulton, to whom we were very loyal. In those days it was a show of respect that no one who knew her would think of using her first name, and I have no memory of ever hearing it. I was fortunate to have this enforced contact with her because she was a humble, honest, and utterly devout individual. Although she had one eye that would not open and was crippled with arthritis almost to the point of being unable to walk, she was completely free in her mental ability to turn to God.

Because she didn't give the appearance of being a successful practitioner, Mrs. Fulton did not have the admiration of those in her religion who did not know her. In fact, she was often looked down on because she had not healed herself of her own physical ailments. Yet she was obviously unconcerned with what others thought of her and also unconcerned with the relative poverty in which she seemed to live. She had a deep and immediate sense of the oneness of God, and this was really all that mattered to her. Although I went to her primarily because of her effortless ability to heal, what affected me most deeply was the simplicity with which she turned to God. After listening to what I had to say, she would merely close her eyes and, under her breath, say this little prayer:

> *I am one with Thee,*
> *Oh Thou infinite One.*
> *I am where Thou art.*
> *I am what Thou art.*
> *I am because Thou art.*

I don't know if it was entirely her influence or if I also came into the world this way, but for as long as I can remember, I have had a persistent yearning to return to God. The feeling is almost like homesickness, except that it is not sad. It's more like a warm, lovely memory buried deep in my mind, a memory of the time we all once knew and that nothing in this world can replace. No matter how far I strayed in my life — and I strayed into the gutters more than once — my yearning for God has always gently lifted me from whatever destructive path I was on and given me back the single concern of coming home.

Early in our long marriage, Gayle and I developed a deep conviction about the way we should perceive our lives in relation to God. Our goal has been to seek God for the sake of God and for no other reason. We learned we cannot expect that, as a result of this effort, the world will somehow work better for us. To the extent we slip into thinking that God (or Truth) can be used, we become confused and disillusioned with life. In fact, discouragement always seems to signal some form of this mistake.

This is the two-part principle we come back to again and again: First, we must take up our life as our life is today. We must commit to the bodies that we have, to the children we have, to where we live and work, even to the physical symptoms we have this instant and to whatever mess we have caused that we find ourselves in today. In other words, we commit to our mistakes as well as to the mistakes of others. We see them clearly and recognize them as part of our path home — even as we take steps to stop making the mistakes.

The second part is that no matter what the picture of our life is, we must turn to God anyway. In every small encounter, in every detail of every circumstance, we must turn to God. And we must keep doing this until each activity becomes a prayer. Cleaning up the dog hair, balancing the checkbook, waiting for someone who is late, firing an employee, saying yes, saying no — whatever we find before us is nothing more than an opportunity to know the peace of God. Not a code of conduct, it does not look a certain way — it feels a certain way.

How our lives appear to be working does not indicate the quality or extent of our efforts. Surely this should be obvious; yet so often we take our devotion and scatter it across the picture of our lives. We seek God and then turn to circumstances for confirmation. There is little connection between the process and the outcome — cruelly motivated people end up in nice circumstances and vice versa — but it is only in the process that God can be seen.

When we recognize that nothing has to go right for us to be happy, that people do not have to behave for us to love them, our walk home can become surprisingly simple. We have enormous power not to manipulate the world, but to be happy and to know peace. The secret to finding God is understanding that there is no great spiritual attainment that must come first. Anyone who wants to feel God's presence will feel God's presence.

How people develop their awareness of God, the methods they use, is almost irrelevant because each person will have a sense of how best to proceed. With some it can start through meditation. Others may use a traditional form of prayer. Some will feel God's presence through service to a particular group by doing no more than committing themselves to their spouses, their children, their families. When we look into our hearts and ask, "How can I begin to experience my goodness? How can I make the effort today to be the kind of person I want to be?" we will have some sense of how to begin, and that sense will be sufficient.

One procedure is, first thing on rising, to set a simple purpose for the day, for example, to look at all living things the way we sense God sees them. Specific times for recalling our purpose can be scheduled, such as pausing every time the car ignition is turned on and off. To this can be added a longer meditation at some feasible point in the day. And then, just before going to sleep, schedule a moment to release the day, to release the mind of anything still carried that does not contribute to an innocent vision.

The particular means one uses does not matter, but to have a method, a plan, a specific spiritual program is very helpful. Simply begin with your heart, look deeply into it, and trust what you feel. Practice knowing and you will know.

Ultimately, it is not a question of learning something we don't already know, but of beginning with what we believe. What we believe will take us to God very quickly — if practiced daily. The fatal mistake is waiting for life's circumstances to be right before we begin. We wait for the right partner, the right income, the right degree of health, the right time of day. We have already wasted thousands of years waiting for circumstances to be right. And yet some of the holiest people in the world have become so within the most adverse circumstances. The only difference between them and us is that they did not wait to begin.

When we feel the peace of God there is no question about what we are feeling. And when we feel genuine peace, it is obvious when we are not feeling it — we experience a miserable jolt whenever we judge someone, or become "justifiably" angry or selfish and withdrawn, or anything else contrary to the leadings of our hearts. Even small betrayals of ourselves or others have devastating results. In other words, our tolerance for not experiencing God vanishes.

Sometimes, when we are attempting to walk this path, not only does life not become easier, but it seems to get harder. Of course, this is not actually occurring. It is just that the mistakes we got away with before affect us now because we have experienced a different state.

What we are experiencing never needs to be analyzed. If we wonder whether we are feeling the peace of God, we are not. If we wonder whether we have forgiven someone, we have not. Only the ego judges progress and compares one day's peace with another day's peace. To get caught up in the question of how we are doing is to decide against God *now*. Discouragement is merely love of the ego, because we turn to the ego as the alternative to God's peace.

Another confusing phenomenon as we journey home is a certain smoothing out of external difficulties. As we experience peace we will be less demanding in the relationships we have and less confused as to whose company to seek in the future. Consequently, chronic relationship problems may dissolve. Likewise, as seeking peace becomes more important to us, we will make more peaceful decisions about our finances, our health, and so on, and chronic problems in these areas may also dissolve. But this does not mean that the mind can be used to acquire or that the ego's current notion of what is ideal physically is a part of spiritual gain. It is also possible that one's relationships, finances, and health may seem to deteriorate. As long as God, and not circumstances, is our preoccupation, however, these changes in the external picture will not constitute a side road.

Even when our hearts turn to God, and want only God, we still must deal with the world and make the best decisions we can. However, no longer will devotion be held within isolated compartments of our lives to be exercised only at certain times of day and only under certain circumstances. All activities and decisions will become a spiritual practice, and the reward will be that we made the decision with God. Now, all we could ever want, and certainly all we could ever receive, is "just a closer walk with Thee."

Compassion in Action

by MOTHER TERESA

❧

"The fruit of love is service, which is compassion in action."

TO ME, GOD AND COMPASSION are one and the same. Compassion is the joy of sharing. It's doing small things for the love of each other — just a smile, or carrying a bucket of water, or showing some simple kindness. These are the small things that make up compassion.

Compassion means trying to share and understand the suffering of people. And I think it's very good when people suffer. To me, that's really like the kiss of Jesus. And a sign, also, that this person has come so close to Jesus, sharing his passion.

It is only pride and selfishness and coldness that keep us from having compassion. When we ultimately go home to God, we are going to be judged on what we were to each other, what we did for each other, and, especially, how much love we put in that. It's not how much we give, but how much love we put in the *doing* — that's compassion in action.

One's religion has nothing to do with compassion. It's our love for God that is the main thing. Many Christians and non-Christians alike come to help in our houses in Calcutta and throughout the world. We have volunteers of all religions working with our aides day and night. Religion is meant to help us come closer to God, not meant to separate us...true religion, no? All God really wants is for us to love Him. The way we can show our love for Him is to serve others.

You may ask how the contemplative life fits together with compassion in action. It fits together by bringing union with God. Jesus said, "Whatever you do to the last of my brethren, you are doing it to me." If you do everything for Him, you are acting as a contemplative in the heart of the world.

There is the contemplative life where people separate themselves completely from the world and live a life of prayer, of sacrifice. We are out in the world doing that — being contemplatives in the heart of the world.

We need a life of deep prayer to be able to give until it hurts. It seems the more we have, the less we give. And the less we have, the more we can give.

The need is great for food, clothes, medicine, and tender-love-and-care. This is the greatest need. We have homes for the dying, for lepers, for children, for the poorest of the poor. And now, in the United States, we have homes for people with AIDS also.

My message to the people of today is simple. We must

love one another as God loves each one of us. To be able to love, we need a clean heart. Prayer is what gives us a clean heart. The fruit of prayer is a deepening of faith and the fruit of faith is love. The fruit of love is service, which is compassion in action.

Religion has nothing to do with compassion; it is our love for God that is the main thing because we have all been created for the sole purpose to love and be loved.

Afterword

T HE CONTRIBUTORS TO THIS ANTHOLOGY share with us the understanding that our experience of God is a process of continual unfolding. We are daily recreating our relationship with God with our faith and in our actions. It is a process of allowing ourselves to be clear, seeing God reflected in all the experiences of life and its creations, especially ourselves. For some of us, a single event acts as the catalyst and major source of insight for our spiritual dimension. For others, a more gradual awakening takes place over a lifetime. In either case, every activity, every communication, and every venture is a reaffirmation of our personal relationship with God.

Rather than attempting to define God, we may cultivate an observance of God in action in our daily lives. God can be seen all around us when we quiet our minds enough to listen — when we open our hearts to the beauty that is before us. God doesn't change, for it is what it is. What does change is our own understanding. In one instant we can see God in a child in the next, a beautiful sunset. Everything within us as well as everything around us becomes a mirror of God.

We may consider the possibility that God is not something separate from ourselves, but a part of us. As the authors in this collection explain, God is always present and does not need to be "found," but rather the obstructions keeping us from experiencing God need to be taken away. There is no place and there is no time that God is ever absent; just places and times where we may fail to be aware of God's presence. We find God by looking within and by looking all around us.

Embracing God is an act of embracing ourselves as well as embracing the circle of life all around us. We will all find our personal truth as how to best do this. We do not have to search to embrace God, for God's presence is already with us. The authors suggest that we can embrace God through presence, kindness, work, love, compassion, humility, prayer, community, and gratitude. We do not have to wait for a particular time or place to best embrace God, but simply create the space in our lives for God to enter. There is no less of God found in a single flower than in a church or synagogue. We need not embrace God out of a sense of fear or dogma or reward, but to realize the divinity that we are a part of and that is a part of us. We find that each activity becomes a prayer and that, through us, God is always present.

There are many paths to discover what some may call God, others the dharma or truth, and others the Great Spirit. The contributors suggest that the quest for this discovery may best be sought through our own inner experiences. The tools for discovering God exist for us at every moment: By being present and mindful, by opening our hearts, by softening our ego boundaries, by being aware of our senses and emotions, we can discover the truth and the divine that has always existed for us. No two persons will travel the same path of discovery. However, there will be much common ground as we leave ourselves open to discover the wonders and beauty of God. With time our understanding of God increases to include all of humanity, even cultures and people who are vastly different from ourselves. And as each of us travels on our separate journeys, we may realize that this is the purpose for which we took birth: to discover God, to discover truth, to discover ourselves.

RICHARD CARLSON, PH.D.
P.O. Box 1196
Orinda, CA 94563

BENJAMIN SHIELD, PH.D.
2118 Wilshire Boulevard, Suite 741
Santa Monica, CA 90403

About the Contributors

A.H. ALMAAS

A.H. Almaas is the pen name of A. Hameed Ali, the originator of the Diamond Approach. Born in Kuwait, his academic background is in physics, mathematics, and psychology. He discovered that the ego, or personality, is not only an impediment to growth and happiness but also covers up the vital aspects we need to feel fulfilled. Aspects of this development are explored in his 1995 book *Luminous Night's Journey*. In 1975, Ali founded the Ridhwan School in Boulder, Colorado, and Berkeley, California. The school now has about 900 members around the United States and abroad, with students in Canada, Australia, Germany, the Netherlands, Great Britain, and other countries. In 1986, he founded Diamond Books, which now publishes his writing as A.H. Almaas and also makes available video and audiotapes of his teaching. His latest book is *The Point of Existence: Transformations of Narcissism in Self-Realization*. Ali now lives in Berkeley, California.

REVEREND MICHAEL BECKWITH

Rev. Michael Beckwith is the founder/minister of the Agape International Center of Truth in Santa Monica, California, home of the Agape Church of Religious Science. (Agape is the Greek word for unconditional love.) The Agape Church is one of the largest multicultural spiritual communities of its kind in the United States and is dedicated to the realization of the presence of God, peace, and love on this planet. In addition to speaking each Sunday and Wednesday at the Agape Center, Rev. Michael travels as a guest speaker, workshop leader, and facilitator of meditation retreats throughout the world. He has served in many leadership positions in the New Thought movement and is presently dean and director of the School of Ministry at Ernest Holmes College. In February 1995, he was awarded a Doctorate of Divinity by the United Church of Religious Science. Rev. Michael has written articles for *Science of Mind* magazine, the *International New Thought Alliance* magazine, and other publications. In October 1993, Rev. Michael started publishing *Inner Visions* magazine, a daily meditation booklet, supported by the Agape Licensed Practitioners. He appears on radio and television in the Los Angeles area and nationally. Rev. Michael and the Agape Church are the recipients of numerous awards for community development and humanitarian work.

SUE BENDER

Formerly a teacher and family therapist, Sue Bender is now a ceramic artist, bestselling author, and much sought-after lecturer nationwide. She holds a B.A. from Simmons College, an M.A. from the Harvard University School of Education, and a Master's in Social Work from the University of California at Berkeley. During her active years as a family therapist, Bender was founder and director of CHOICE: The Institute of the Middle Years. Bender is the author of *Plain and Simple: A Woman's Journey to the Amish* (HarperSanFrancisco), a *New York Times* bestseller with over 400,000 copies sold, which describes her experiences living among the Amish and their seemingly timeless world — a journey inspired by her fascination with Amish quilts. In *Everyday Sacred: A Woman's Journey Home* (HarperSanFrancisco), Bender chronicles her struggle to bring the simplicity and joy she experienced with the Amish back to her hectic days at home. Bender is a ceramic artist whose work has been shown in museums and galleries nationwide. She lives in Berkeley, California, with her husband Richard, and is the mother of two grown sons.

JEAN SHINODA BOLEN, M.D.

Jean Shinoda Bolen, M.D., is a Jungian analyst and clinical professor of psychiatry at the University of California, San Francisco. She is an internationally renowned lecturer and workshop leader and a fellow of the American Psychiatric Association (APA). She is a past chairperson of the Council of National Affairs of the APA and a former member of the Board of the *Ms.* Foundation for Women. She was one of twenty-two women in the 1986 Academy Award-winning antinuclear documentary *Women—For America, For the World* and appeared in *Goddess Remembered,* the first of the Canadian Film Board's trilogy on women's spirituality. Her books include *The Tao of Psychology, Goddesses in Everywoman, Gods in Everyman, Ring of Power, Crossing to Avalon,* and *Close to the Bone: Life-Threatening Illness and the Search for Meaning.* She lives in Mill Valley, California, and practices in San Francisco.

THE DALAI LAMA

His Holiness the Dalai Lama, Tenzin Gyatso, is the head of state and spiritual leader of the Tibetan people. He was born Lhamo Dhondrub on July 6, 1935, in a small village called Taktser in northeastern Tibet. Born to a peasant family, His Holiness was recognized at the age of two, in accordance with Tibetan tradition, as the reincarnation of his predecessor, the 13th Dalai Lama, and thus an incarnation of Avalokitesvara, the Buddha of Compassion. In 1959, nine years after China invaded Tibet, he went into exile to Dharamsala, India, where he lives today as leader of the Tibetan government in exile. Numerous Western universities and institutions have conferred honorary degrees and awards in recognition of his writings and activism for peace, human rights, and environmentalism. He travels throughout the world, cutting across religious, national, and political barriers, speaking on peace and compassion. He won the Nobel Peace Prize in 1989.

BARBARA DE ANGELIS, PH.D.

Barbara De Angelis, Ph.D., is one of America's leading

experts on relationships, and a highly respected leader in the field of personal growth. Barbara is the author of five best-selling books, which have sold over four million copies and been published in twenty languages. Her first book, *How to Make Love All the Time*, was a national bestseller. Her next two books, *Secrets About Men Every Woman Should Know* and *Are You the One for Me?* were #1 on the *New York Times* bestseller list for months. Her fourth book, *Real Moments*, also became an overnight *New York Times* bestseller, and was followed by *Real Moments for Lovers*. Her most recent books are *Confidence, Ask Barbara*, and *The Real Rules*. She writes regularly for magazines including *Cosmopolitan, Ladies Home Journal, McCalls, Readers Digest, Redbook*, and *Family Circle*. Barbara appeared weekly for two years on CNN as their Newsnight Relationship Expert, and has hosted her own daily television show for CBS TV and her own radio talk show in Los Angeles. She has been a frequent guest on the *Oprah Winfrey Show, Donahue, LEEZA*, and *Geraldo*, as well as a regular contributor to *Entertainment Tonight*. Barbara was the founder of the Los Angeles Personal Growth Center and its executive director for twelve years. She is now president of Shakti Communications, Inc., which provides production and consulting services. She lives in Southern California with her husband, Dr. Jeffrey James, their two dogs, and a cat.

WAYNE DYER, PH.D.

Dr. Wayne Dyer is one of the most widely read authors in the field of personal growth. He is the author of eleven books, including the bestselling *Your Erroneous Zones*, which has sold over six million copies, *Pulling Your Own Strings*, and *The Sky's the Limit*. He has also written *What Do You Really Want for Your Children, No More Holiday Blues* (a novel), *Gifts from Eykis, You'll See It When You Believe It, Real Magic, Everyday Wisdom, Your Sacred Self*, and *Staying on the Path*. His most recent book is *Manifest Your Destiny: The Nine Spiritual Principles for Getting Everything You Want*. A psychotherapist, Dyer has a doctorate in counseling psychology. He has taught at many levels of education, from high school to the teaching hospital of the Cornell University

Medical College. He has coauthored three textbooks and numerous professional journal articles. He lectures across the country to groups numbering in the thousands and appears regularly on radio and television. Dr. Dyer lives with his family in southern Florida.

RIANE EISLER

Riane Eisler is an internationally acclaimed scholar, futurist, and activist. She is codirector, with her husband, social scientist David Loye, of the Center for Partnership Studies in Pacific Grove, California. She is a cultural historian whose multidisciplinary approach incorporates evolutionary studies, feminism, human rights, and peace activism. She is the author of the groundbreaking work of women's studies and history *The Chalice and the Blade: Our History, Our Future,* which has sold over 500,000 copies and been hailed by anthropologist Ashley Montagu as "the most important book since Darwin's *Origin of Species.*" She is also the author of *The Partnership Way,* with David Loye, and *Sacred Pleasure: Sex, Myth, and the Politics of the Body.*

MATTHEW FOX, PH.D.

Matthew Fox is the founder and president of the University of Creation Spirituality in Oakland, California. He is best-known for the recovery of the Creation Spirituality tradition, which brings together ecology, cosmology, justice, and mysticism in a theology based on "original blessing." Fox is the author of twenty-two books on culture and spirituality, including *Original Blessing, Illuminations of Hildegard of Bingen, The Reinvention of Work,* and *Confessions,* his spiritual autobiography. He holds his Ph.D. in the history and theology of spirituality from the Institute Catholique in Paris and was formerly a Dominican priest. He has been an Episcopalian priest since 1994. In 1995, he was awarded The Peace Abbey Courage of Conscience Award.

SHAKTI GAWAIN

Shakti Gawain is a bestselling author and internationally

renowned speaker and workshop leader in the world consciousness movement. She is the author of many bestsellers, including *The Path of Transformation: How Healing Ourselves Can Change the World*, *Creative Visualization*, which has more than 2 million copies in print, and *Living in the Light*, which has more than 700,000 copies in print. Her latest book is *Creating True Prosperity*. She has appeared on such nationally syndicated shows as the *Oprah Winfrey Show*, *Good Morning America*, *Sonya Live on CNN*, *LEEZA*, and the *Larry King Show*. She has helped thousands of people to learn, develop, and act on their own intuition and creativity. She is cofounder, with her husband, Jim Burns, of Nataraj Publishing, and was cofounder of New World Library. She lives in Mill Valley, California, and on the island of Kauai, Hawaii.

JOSEPH GOLDSTEIN

Joseph Goldstein graduated from Columbia College in 1965 with a B.A. in Philosophy. He served two years as a Peace Corps volunteer in Bangkok, Thailand, where he became interested in Buddhism and meditation. He spent most of the following seven years in India, studying and practicing Vipassana (Insight) meditation. In 1976 he cofounded the Insight Meditation Center in Barre, Massachusetts, where he is one of the resident guiding teachers. In 1984, he began further study under the guidance of Ven. U Pandita Sayadaw, one of the great meditation masters of Burma. He is the author of *The Experience of Insight: A Simple and Direct Guide to Buddhist Meditation* and coauthor, with Jack Kornfield, of *Seeking the Heart of Wisdom: The Path of Insight Meditation*.

THICH NHAT HANH

A rare combination of mystic, scholar, and activist monk, Thich Nhat Hanh was born in 1926 in Vietnam. He entered the monkhood at age sixteen and has since become one of the West's most recognized and beloved Zen Buddhist teachers. A pioneer in the concept of engaged Buddhism, he was chairman of the Buddhist Peace Delegation during the Vietnam War. His role in opposing the war earned him both a nomination from Dr. Martin Luther King, Jr. for the Nobel Peace Prize and exile from his homeland since 1966. He is the author of over twenty-five books, including *Peace Is Every Step*, and *The Miracle of Mindfulness*. His most recent bestseller, *Living Buddha, Living Christ*, explores the crossroads of two great religious figures and their traditions. Thich Nhat Hanh lives in exile in France, where he leads his Tiep Hien Order (Order of Interbeing).

ANDREW HARVEY

Andrew Harvey is a renowned writer, lecturer, and teacher. An Englishman born in India in 1952, Harvey was educated at Oxford and, at 21, became a Fellow of All Soul's College. In 1977, he returned to India and began a lifelong spiritual quest, studying and practicing Hindu mysticism at the ashram of Sri Aurobindo and learning from Tibetan Buddhist teacher Thuksey Rinpoche and from the Christian mystic and prophet Bede Griffiths. Returning to teach in Europe and America, Harvey continued his explorations with extensive study in Eastern and Western mystical literature. Harvey is the author of two spiritual autobiographies, *A Journey to Ladakh* and *Hidden Journey*. His interpretations and translations of the work of the thirteenth-century Sufi mystical poet Rumi have appeared in *Love's Fire, Speaking Flame, The Way of Passion, Light Upon Light*, and *Love's Glory*. His recent work includes two anthologies, *The Essential Mystics* and *The Essential Gay Mystics*. He is currently at work on a book about Christ. Harvey lives with his husband, writer and photographer Eryk Hanut, in Nevada. Their recent collaboration, *Mary's Vineyard: Daily Meditations, Readings, Revelations*, won a 1997 Benjamin Franklin Award.

BARBARA MARX HUBBARD

Barbara Marx Hubbard is an author, futurist, social architect, lecturer, and visionary. She has spent the last thirty years identifying options and people contributing to a creative, sustainable future. In the 1970s and 1980s, she worked on designing and producing major synergistic conferences, bringing together opposing factions to seek cooperative solutions, such as the Soviet-American Citizen Summits to develop joint-nation projects. She has worked closely with such thinkers as Buckminster Fuller, Hazel Henderson, Virginia Satir, Ray Bradbury, Jonas Salk, and Norman Cousins. In 1984, her name was placed in nomination for the vice presidency of the United States with her "campaign for a positive future." She is the author of *The Hunger for Eve, The Evolutionary Journey, The Revelation: A Message of Hope for the New Millennium,* and, most recently, *Conscious Evolution: Awakening Our Social Potential.* She lives in Marin County, California.

Gerald Jampolsky, M.D.

Gerald Jampolsky, M.D., is a psychiatrist, author, and founder of the Center for Attitudinal Healing, which he started in 1975 to provide emotional support for people with catastrophic illness. His books include the international bestseller *Love Is Letting Go of Fear, Goodbye to Guilt,* and *Love Is the Answer,* which he co-wrote with his wife Diane V. Cirincione. His most recent book is *Listen to Me,* which he co-wrote with his psychologist son, Lee Jampolsky, about father-son relationships. Dr. Jampolsky is a noted child and adult psychiatrist and is the recipient of many awards, including the Caring Award, given to the ten most caring people in the U.S., and the Sadat Peace Prize.

Rabbi Harold Kushner, Ph.D.

Rabbi Harold Kushner, Ph.D., is a rabbi laureate of Temple Israel in Natick, Massachusetts, where he has served since 1966. He is best known for his book *When Bad Things Happen to Good People,* an international bestseller first published in 1981. The book has been translated into twelve languages and was selected by the Book-of-the-Month Club as one of the ten most influential books of recent years. He has also written *When All You've Ever Wanted Isn't Enough,* which was awarded the Christopher medal in 1987 for its contribution to the exaltation of the human spirit, *When Children Ask About God, Who Needs God?, To*

Life!, and his most recent bestseller, *How Good Do We Have to Be?*
Rabbi Kushner is a native of Brooklyn, New York, and was educated at Columbia University and the Jewish Theological Seminary, where he was ordained in 1960 and received his doctorate
in 1972.

STEPHEN LEVINE

Stephen Levine is a poet and teacher of guided meditation
and healing techniques that have found widespread application over the past twenty years. He edited the *San Francisco Oracle* in the late 1960s. After intense practice of Mindfulness
Meditation under the tutelage of an American Buddhist monk,
Levine edited the *Mindfulness Series* for Unity Press. For the past
twenty years Levine and his wife, Ondrea, have worked with the
terminally ill and people in crisis. He is the author of several
bestselling books, including *Who Dies?*, *Healing into Life and
Death*, and *A Gradual Awakening*. He is the coauthor of *Grist for
the Mill* (with Ram Dass), and of *Embracing the Beloved* (with his
wife, Ondrea). His most recent book is *A Year to Live: How to Live
This Year As If It Were Your Last*. The Levines live in northern
New Mexico.

FATHER WILLIAM MCNAMARA

Father William McNamara was born in Providence, Rhode
Island. He became a Discalced Carmelite monk in 1944 and was
ordained a Roman Catholic priest in 1951. Since then Father
William has been a lecturer and retreat master in Canada, Ireland, and the United States. In 1960, after an audience with
Pope John XXIII, Father William founded the Spiritual Life
Institute, and established hermitages in Sedona, Arizona, and
Crestone, Colorado. Both centers pray the Divine Office, the
traditional Prayer of the Church. Readings for the meditation
are taken from the great religious traditions of the world:
Sufism, Hinduism, Taoism, and Zen Buddhism. Father William
is the author of *Art of Being Human*, *The Human Adventure: The
Art of Contemplative Living*, and *Mystical Passion: The Art of Christian Loving*.

Brooke Medicine Eagle

Brooke Medicine Eagle is a Native American earth wisdom teacher, singer, ceremonial leader, sacred ecologist, and author of *Buffalo Woman Comes Singing*, in which she explores Native American rituals like the medicine wheel. A Lakota raised on the Crow reservation in Montana, she is a licensed counselor, practitioner of Neuro-Linguistic Programming, and certified Feldenkrais practitioner. She lives in the Flathead Valley of Montana, is the creator of Eagle Song, a series of spiritually oriented wilderness camps, and is the founder of the FlowerSong Project, which promotes a sustainable, ecologically sound path upon Mother Earth for seven generations of children.

Howard Murphet

Howard Murphet has been a journalist, teacher, copywriter, freelance writer, and industrial public relations officer, in addition to being the primary biographer of Sai Baba. Born in 1906 in Tasmania, Australia, during World War II he served as a British army officer in the invasions of Sicily and Italy, as well as the D-Day invasion of Normandy. He later headed the British press corps at the Nuremberg trials. In 1964, Murphet began a six-year stay in India, during which he studied Yoga and Hindi spiritual practices under Sachisai Baba. He is the author of *Sai Baba: Man of Miracles*, *When Daylight Comes: A Biography of Helena Petrovna Blavatsky*, *Walking the Path with Sai Baba*, and *Sai Inner Views and Insights*.

Hugh Prather

Hugh Prather, with his wife Gayle, is the author of eleven books, including *Notes to Myself* (which has more than five million copies in print), *Notes on Love and Courage*, and *A Book for Couples*. He has been called "an American Kahlil Gibran" by the *New York Times* and "one of the most compelling, insightful, inspirational, spiritual authors of our time" by *New Realities* magazine. The Prathers live in Tucson, Arizona, where they are resident ministers at St. Francis in the Foothills Methodist Church. Their latest book is *Spiritual Parenting: A Guide to Understanding and Nurturing the Heart of Your Child*. Their greatest joy is their three sons.

ANN WILSON SCHAEF, PH.D.

Ann Wilson Schaef, Ph.D., is a world-renowned lecturer, organizational consultant, former psychotherapist, and author. She is president of Wilson Schaef Associates, Inc. She has appeared on national television and radio shows and lectures at major conventions, universities, and conferences throughout the world. She is the author of numerous books, including *The Addictive Organization*; *Beyond Therapy, Beyond Science: A New Model for Healing the Whole Person*; *Co-Dependence: Misunderstood, Mistreated*; *When Society Becomes an Addict*; *Women's Reality: An Emerging Female System in a White Male Society*; and the bestselling *Meditations for Women Who Do Too Much*. She lives in Montana and Hawaii.

MARSHA SINETAR

Corporate psychologist Marsha Sinetar is a pioneering educator whose books are used worldwide in colleges, churches, and corporate and counseling settings. Aside from the occasional lecture or corporate project, she enjoys a reflective writer's life in the San Juan Islands of the Pacific Northwest. Her writing focuses on the spiritual dimension of adult growth and work. She is the author of the million-copy bestseller *Do What You Love, The Money Will Follow: Discovering Your Right Livelihood*; its sequel, *To Build the Life You Want, Create the Work You Love: The Spiritual Dimension of Entrepreneuring*; as well as *Developing a 21st Century Mind*; and *Ordinary People As Monks and Mystics: Lifestyles for Self-Discovery*.

HUSTON SMITH, PH.D.

Huston Smith is widely regarded as one of the most eloquent and accessible authorities on the philosophy of comparative religion and the history of religion. His teaching career — which includes time at Washington University, M.I.T., and Syracuse University — has been devoted to bridging intellectual gulfs: between East and West, between science and the humanities, and between formal and popular education. He is professor emeritus of religious studies at Syracuse University and was visiting professor at the University of California, Berkeley. His classic work of comparative religion, *The World's Religions*, has sold over 1.5 million copies. He was recently featured in conversation with Bill Moyers in *The Wisdom of Faith*, a PBS series in which he explored Hinduism, Buddhism, Confucianism, Taoism, Christianity, Judaism, and Islam.

Brother David Steindl-Rast, Ph.D.

Brother David Steindl-Rast became a Benedictine monk at Mount Saviour Monastery in New York state in 1953. Born in Vienna, Brother Steindl-Rast holds degrees from the Vienna Academy of Fine Arts and the Psychological Institute at the University of Vienna. He was a Post-Doctoral Fellow at Cornell University. He periodically goes on retreats at Immaculate Heart Hermitage in Big Sur, California. After twelve years of formal training in philosophy, theology, and the 1,500-year-old Benedictine monastic tradition, he received permission to practice Zen meditation with Buddhist masters. His books include *Gratefulness, The Heart of Prayer, A Listening Heart*, and *The Ground We Share: Everyday Practice, Buddhist and Christian*, with Robert Aitken.

Mother Teresa

Mother Teresa became known to the world for selfless work with the "poorest of the poor" in Calcutta, India. She was born Agnes Boyaxhui in Skopje, now the capital of Macedonia, in 1910. Mother Teresa began her novitiate in India in 1928 and taught high school there for nearly twenty years. Since its inception in 1950, her order, the Missionaries of Charity, has opened more than 500 centers around the world to help the dying and destitute. In 1996, President Bill Clinton signed legislation making her an honorary U.S. citizen. She stepped down as head of her order in 1997. Mother Teresa is the recipient of the many of the world's most prestigious humanitarian awards, including the United States Medal of Freedom, the United Nations Albert Schweitzer Prize, and the Nobel Peace Prize.

MARIANNE WILLIAMSON

Marianne Williamson is an internationally acclaimed author and lecturer in the fields of spirituality and new thought. She teaches the basic principles of *A Course in Miracles* and discusses their application to basic living. All three of her books — *A Return to Love, A Woman's Worth,* and *Illuminata* — have been #1 *New York Times* bestsellers. Ms. Williamson is a native of Houston. She has been lecturing professionally on spirituality and metaphysics since 1983, both in the United States and abroad. She has done extensive charitable organizing throughout the country in service to people with life-challenging illnesses. Her latest book is *The Healing of America.*

About the Editors

RICHARD CARLSON, PH.D.

Dr. Richard Carlson is a nationally known author who has spoken on happiness to audiences of thousands. His books include the #1 *New York Times* bestseller *Don't Sweat the Small Stuff*, *You Can Be Happy No Matter What*, *You Can Feel Good Again*, *Shortcut Through Therapy*, and *Slowing Down to the Speed of Life* (with Joseph Bailey). His latest book is *Don't Worry, Make Money*. He is the coeditor, with Benjamin Shield, Ph.D., of *Handbook for the Soul*, *Handbook for the Heart*, and *Healers on Healing*. Dr. Carlson is a frequent lecturer who has appeared on hundreds of radio and television shows, including *LEEZA*, *Sally Jesse Raphael*, and the *Oprah Winfrey Show*. He lives with his wife and daughters in Northern California.

BENJAMIN SHIELD, PH.D.

Dr. Benjamin Shield is a therapist, educator, and lecturer practicing in Santa Monica, California, and teaches throughout the United States and Europe. He holds degrees in biochemistry and biology from the University of California, and has performed advanced studies at the Boston University School of Medicine. His doctoral degree is in health sciences. He has been a frequent guest on television and radio talk shows. He was a featured guest on the BBC/Canadian TV series *Medicine or Magic?* and a contributing author to the book *Alternative Medicine*. He believes that healing and spirituality share common denominators and are accessible to each of us. He has authored numerous articles on psychology, healing, and spirituality. He is coeditor, with Richard Carlson, of *Handbook for the Heart*, *Handbook for the Soul*, and *Healers on Healing*.

If you enjoyed *For the Love of God*, we highly recommend these books from New World Library:

No Greater Love by Mother Teresa, with a foreword by Thomas Moore. This definitive volume features Mother Teresa on love, prayer, giving, service, poverty, forgiveness, Jesus, and more. The most accessible and inspirational collection of her writings ever published.

In the Heart of the World by Mother Teresa. A small book of Mother Teresa's inspiring words, divided into thoughts, stories, and prayers. Readers will learn Mother Teresa's philosophies, follow her as she works in the desperate corners of the world, and share her favorite prayers.

The Words of Christ edited by Dale Salwak. This brilliantly edited collection of quotes taken from the four canonical Gospels, the Acts of the Apostles, 1 and 2 Corinthians, and Revelation contains the essential teachings of Jesus, organized thematically.

The Wisdom of Judaism edited by Dale Salwak. Biblical scholar Dale Salwak plumbs the vast teachings of Judaism for its essence in this concise treasury of practical and inspirational Jewish insight. Includes an afterword of quotations from such modern Jewish thinkers as Albert Einstein, Golda Meir, and Margaret Fishback Powers.

You Can Be Happy No Matter What by Richard Carlson, Ph.D. Most of us believe that our happiness depends on outside circumstances. Here, Dr. Carlson clearly shows that happiness has nothing to do with forces beyond our control — and, in fact, our natural state is contentment.

New World Library is dedicated to publishing books
and cassettes that inspire and challenge us
to improve the quality of our lives and our world.

Our books and tapes are available at bookstores
everywhere. For a catalog of our complete library
of books and cassettes, contact:

New World Library
14 Pamaron Way
Novato, CA 94949

Phone: (415) 884-2100
Fax: (415) 884-2199

Or call toll free: (800) 972-6657
Catalog requests: Ext. 900
Ordering: Ext. 902

E-mail: escort@nwlib.com
http://www.nwlib.com